Voices in Refuge

STORIES FROM
SUDANESE REFUGEES IN CAIRO

Edited by
Nora Eltahawy
Brooke Comer
Amani Elshimi

The American University in Cairo Press
Cairo New York

First published in 2009 by
The American University in Cairo Press
113 Sharia Kasr el Aini, Cairo, Egypt
420 Fifth Avenue, New York 10018
www.aucpress.com

Dar el Kutub No. 4199/09
ISBN 978 977 416 305 0

Dar el Kutub Cataloging-in-Publication Data

Eltahawy, Nora
        Voices in Refuge: Stories from Sudanese Refugees in Cairo / Nora Eltahawy.—Cairo:
    The American University in Cairo Press, 2009
        p.   cm.
        ISBN 978 977 416 305 0
        1. Refugees, Sudan—Egypt   I. Title
        325.21096240962

1 2 3 4 5 6 7 8   14 13 12 11 10 09

Designed by Adam el Sehemy
Printed in Egypt

Voices
in
Refuge

Dedicated to all whose voices have been silenced by lives in refuge and to the courageous men and women without whom this project would not have been possible. We thank you for allowing us into your lives, and we stand humbled by your courage.

Contents

Acknowledgments

Our deepest thanks to Dr. Barbara Harrell-Bond for introducing us to many of the refugees interviewed and for her work on the foreword. Thank you to Chris Terry, Randi Danforth, Chip Rossetti, Neil Hewison, and Noha Mohammed for their advice and patience throughout the conception of this manuscript.

Foreword

Barbara Harrell-Bond

I t is a privilege to write the foreword to this impressive collection of refugees voices. It provides an inspiring testimony to the courage of human
beings in overcoming tribulations that go far beyond the daily exigencies
of 'normal' life. It offers a glimpse into unusual families and how, in George's
case, the foresight of a mother in training her children gave him the tools that
allowed him to survive situations the mother could have never envisaged.

In rural sub-Saharan Africa, this mother was probably not unusual, but
George's testimony alerts all of us to the importance of preparing children
for the unexpected in our troubled world. We should all remember when
reading refugee testimonies, this could be me. A problem for you and me is,
as urbanized and largely middle-class readers, we would unlikely be able to
cope with living the life of a refugee; our generation has been de-skilled. Yet
the possibility looms for many of us that one day we could find ourselves in
a situation that required us to seek asylum in a strange land. The life stories
in this book challenge us to think of the courage of people in managing to
cope and survive under extreme hardship.

By embracing the experiences of refugees from Darfur, Khartoum and
southern Sudan, and in one account of a genocide survivor from Burundi,
the reader gains unusual insights into the history of Sudan and the com-
plexities of the civil war that has plagued the country since its independence.
Who would expect that civilians in the south had to fear the 'rebels' (the
Sudanese People's Liberation Army) as much as they had to fear and dodge
the government forces?

Although the Sudanese represent a current majority, they are not the only
nation represented among refugees in Egypt. Readers may not be aware that

Egypt has been a sanctuary for refugees at least from biblical days. In the twentieth century, the time of the beginnings of the 'refugee regime,' it became a place of refuge for Armenians fleeing the 1917–19 genocide in Turkey. Egypt was also one of three governments,[1] from what we today call the 'global south,' to be represented at the drafting of the 1951 United Nations (UN) Refugee Convention, and it was the first non-European government to allow the Office of the United Nations High Commissioner for Refugees (UNHCR) to establish a presence on its territory. This calls for some explanation.

The 1951 Refugee Convention originally applied only to Europeans who fled from their home countries to seek asylum in other European countries in the aftermath of the Second World War. It was believed that once the plight of these victims of the war had been resolved there would be no more refugees; therefore, UNHCR was established as a temporary institution. During the Second World War, Egypt hosted members of several European 'governments in exile.' Among those displaced was an entire camp of Slovenians who needed to be resettled to a country other than Egypt. It was in this context that the 1954 Memorandum of Agreement between Egypt and UNHCR was drawn up, which allowed UNHCR to manage arrangements for European refugees. However, to this day, the document remains in force but has not been amended since its inception. In 1967, the UN refugee Protocol eliminated the geographical limitation to Europe, and extended UNHCR's responsibilities to displaced peoples throughout the world; in time the 1951 Refugee Convention became international law for all those countries which ratified it.

In 1981, Egypt ratified both the 1951 Convention Relating to the Status of Refugees and the 1967 Protocol Relating to the Status of Refugees. According to the 1951 convention, a refugee is "every person who, owing to well-founded fear of being persecuted for reasons of race, religion, nationality, membership of a particular social group or political opinion, is outside the country of his nationality and is unable or, owing to such fear, is unwilling to avail himself of the protection of that country, or who, not having a nationality and being outside the country of his former habitual residence as a result of such events is unable or, owing to such fear, is unwilling to return to it."

Egypt has also ratified the Refugee Convention of the Organization of African Union (now the African Union), which adds Article 2 to this definition, and includes "every person who, owing to external aggression, occupation, foreign domination, or events seriously disturbing public order in either part or the whole of his country of origin or nationality, is compelled to leave his place of habitual residence in order to seek refuge in another place outside his country of origin or nationality." The most important provision of the 1951 Refugee Convention is the prohibition on states from refoulement, or forcibly returning a refugee to a country where he or she fears persecution. This prohibition has now become customary international law, which means it applies even to states that have not ratified the 1951 Convention.

Despite constitutional provisions concerning refugees, the maintenance of Egypt's reservations to the convention, the lack of national laws on refugees, and the unwritten non-integration policy of the Egyptian government have all contributed to the hardships of refugees in Egypt. Moreover, its now unofficial reservations to the 1951 Refugee Convention do not permit refugees to enjoy their basic rights. They are unofficial because when Egypt published the 1951 Refugee Convention and the 1967 Protocol, it did not include the reservations. As yet, no one has brought this matter to the attention of any court on behalf of a refugee, who is being forbidden, for example, to work without a permit.[2]

Today, Egypt hosts refugees from as many as thirty-eight nations—the largest groups are Sudanese, Iraqis, Somalis, Eritreans, and Ethiopians. Many others come from Sub-Saharan African countries, including Rwanda, Burundi, Liberia, Sierra Leone, and Ivory Coast. There are also refugees in Egypt from China, Russia, and many of the republics that were part of the former Soviet Union. The total number of refugees living in Egypt has not been determined. The refugees are not easily counted because they are scattered between the cities of Cairo and Alexandria, the Aswan and Delta regions, and even Sharm al-Sheikh (where some, due to their language skills, are able to find jobs in the tourist industry). In addition, there is no census data to distinguish between them and other foreigners who migrate to Egypt. Moreover, UNHCR, the agency that has taken responsibility for adjudicating their claims for asylum, only recognizes a small number of the refugees. After a refugee has received a negative decision at UNHCR, their file is 'closed.' However, many if not most of the rejected refugees cannot return to their country because they still fear persecution. Egypt hosts thousands of refugees with closed files, who continue to live in the country, albeit illegally.

Some believed that the 2004 Four Freedoms agreement between Egypt and Sudan would resolve the illegality of the presence of such 'closed files' for the Sudanese, but since it requires individuals to cooperate with the Sudanese Embassy, which would essentially amount to refugees re-availing themselves to state protection, it is unlikely that many Sudanese would be prepared to do so. Theoretically, the agreement allows for freedom of movement between Egypt and Sudan and the right to work, own property, and enter into joint ventures. However, thus far, this agreement appears to only operate to the advantage of Egyptians moving to Sudan, as Sudanese must still obtain a visa to enter Egypt.

There are also several vintages of Ethiopians who have migrated to Egypt since the days of the Emperor Haile Selassie. Egypt also received Ethiopian refugees during the Red Terror, the overthrow of Menguistu, and events following, the expulsions of the respective nationals from both countries, and the war between Ethiopia and Eritrea. By 2008, the number of Ethiopian and Eritrean refugees continued to grow as a result of the increased political disturbances in both countries, especially from Ethiopia, since the elections. Large numbers of people, both Eritrean and Ethiopian, escaped to Egypt to avoid the consequences of the evocation of the Cessation Clause in Sudan.[3] Somalis are the next largest group, it is estimated that there are approximately five-thousand Somali refugees living in Egypt and, due to continued unrest in Somalia, that number is growing.

Refugees are often perceived as a threat to the livelihood of poor Egyptians. Although the refugees who tell their stories in this book do not talk a lot about how they make their living, it should be remembered that most of them perform jobs that Egyptians loathe to take on, and that refugees attract remittances from their relatives who are living abroad. Were they allowed to work in the formal sector, their skills would no doubt increase employment opportunities for everyone. It might even change the work ethic of Egypt if everyone were hired on merit.

Unfortunately, the stereotypical view maintains that refugees constitute a burden on Egypt's already overstretched economy; but the opposite is true. The moment any refugee enters a country he or she is immediately a consumer of local products. Refugees pour millions of Egyptian pounds into the housing market because they have to compete for private accommodation along with every other foreigner. As noted, they attract remittances from relatives who are abroad—notably, there has been an increase in the number of Western Union offices in neighborhoods where refugees are concentrated.

Those who migrate to Egypt, much like those who migrate to other economies, typically take jobs that nationals do not want. For example, Egyptian women prefer to do piece work in factories rather than domestic work, so refugees can find jobs as cooks, housekeepers, or nannies. Extra labor in the construction industry also appears to be needed since men are sometimes able to get employment in this sector. But life is still a struggle for sheer survival—probably most refugees are unemployed, underemployed, or exploited for their work by being paid lower salaries than Egyptian workers can command.

As difficult as it is for refugees to have a life in Cairo, the plight of unaccompanied refugee children is even more problematic. Although there are no official figures, those who work with refugees suggest that there are as many as 300 unaccompanied child refugees living in Egypt. This population is extremely vulnerable: they are young and have escaped from violence and persecution, witnessed or lived through horrific events, and upon arrival to Egypt they are alone, unsupported, unprotected, and in exile. The quality of life for the children of refugees living in Cairo is lacking in terms of education and health services. In addition, their lives remain generally insecure, especially with the growing gang violence in the streets of Cairo. These children find themselves at risk of psychological, emotional, physical, and sexual abuse, neglect, and racism as well as economic and sexual exploitation. In their attempts to make a living, girls and young women are vulnerable and often encounter abusive and exploitative behavior. Health and security problems for many unaccompanied minors in Cairo have become familiar features of their daily lives.

For the children, who are mostly from rural backgrounds, the urban setting in Cairo presents an unfamiliar and intimidating terrain. The protection for these children, who find themselves alone, is either insufficient and inconsistent, or sometimes nonexistent. Services for these children are often difficult to locate and access. One's access to these services is also dependent upon the individual's legal status, language abilities, and religion, as well as his or her gender, knowledge and understanding of the city, and ability to express oneself and so on. In 2007, UNHCR provided a minimal monthly stipend to unaccompanied minors, currently LE 170 (around US$32). Unaccompanied minors receive the stipend only if they successfully claim refugee status and are able to overcome numerous bureaucratic obstacles. The UNHCR funds are inadequate to meet a child's subsistence needs, and are automatically terminated when the recipient becomes 18 years old. According to a new policy, children who are unaccompanied by their parents but accompanied by an older brother or sister will lose their stipend once their older sibling reaches the age of eighteen.

Egyptian authorities would be wise to recognize that in order to prevent refugees from becoming an economic burden in the long run, they must be given assistance and opportunities to integrate and ultimately contribute to Egyptian society. By offering social services to these children, and most importantly by educating them, the government would play a significant role in preparing these children to make meaningful contributions to Egyptian society in the future. It is also likely that refugee children who are given access to social services and educational opportunities will be much less likely to resort to criminal activities in order to secure a living.

I congratulate the inspired instructors who introduced this topic to their classes, the students who managed to gain the trust of their 'refugees' to write together such vivid accounts of their experiences, and the refugees who were willing to give of their time to provide us a glimpse of their challenging lives. I especially congratulate the American University in Cairo Press for making this publication available to the public and hope this book will become an annual event.

Introduction

Voices in Refuge reflects the voices of individuals bound together by dislocation, nationality, and history. It presents stories, relayed by Sudanese refugees to a group of students at the American University in Cairo, that go beyond the image of refugees as victims, and deals with issues as varied as the government, non-state actors, civil society, marriage, religious strife, and family values. Through the perspectives of the young and old, male and female, Muslim and Christian, and mother and father, the stories transcend the horrors of genocide to demonstrate a more shared human experience—an experience, we hope will counter the apathy with which Sudan's trauma has been regarded.

The stories here humanize a marginalized group by sharing the individual voices, personalities, and most of all, identities of the refugees. But the volume does more, because the very process of illumination dispels myths that inform the public perception of who refugees are and why they are in Cairo. The frame of reference that most Egyptians draw from is composed of several key myths: that refugees are primitive Africans who can never transcend their second-class status; that they are uneducated, or ineducable; that they have always been destitute, thus their chances for economic prosperity are nil; and that they compete with Egyptians for economic benefit. In Voices in Refuge, we learn of refugees who come from the middle and upper classes, who are lawyers, and the children of doctors. We encounter refugees who, despite their poverty in Sudan, describe a life of peace and happiness in the pre-war period. For all of these, the flight to Egypt was a means of survival, not a search for economic opportunity.

1

The truth that this book tells is that African refugees in Cairo are a potent force, whose talent, experience, and dedication could do much to benefit their host country or their own countries, should they find it possible to return home one day. The poignant detail and nuance with which they describe their homeland suggests a deeply rooted patriotism. Few want to stay in Cairo, where they are unwelcome visitors. Given the chance, they would go home. But political instability and the lack of infrastructure make this impossible for many. The narratives here are told by vibrant, intelligent people, who are rendered invisible by their hosts, and who will likely remain invisible until their stories are brought to light to reveal who they are and what they might become.

The stories were collected over two periods, in the fall of 2006 and 2007, with the consent of the interviewees. The names of the refugees have been changed to protect their identities:

Bahja, a 37-year-old mother of six and native of Darfur, lost several family members at the hands of Janjaweed militants. After being attacked by both the Janjaweed and Sudanese police forces, Bahja was separated from her husband and, with the help of a UN official, crossed the border to Egypt.

Ihsan, grew up in an all-women family and learned the skills of coffee-cup fortune reading and hair braiding as a child. Later, as she struggled to survive as a maid in Cairo, the skills she learned proved invaluable.

Joseph, the son of a prosperous doctor, grew up with arguably more privilege than the millions of Egyptians who look down on him as a black-skinned refugee. His family was ensconced in the upper echelons of Sudanese society. Though he has little in the way of material possessions now, Joseph received an education and benefited from the intellectual ambiance imbued by his father and his friends.

Twenty-three-year-old **Farouq**, who was orphaned at the age of three, has spent most of his life in Egypt. The son of Sudanese refugees, Farouq's experience in Cairo has led him to identify with neither his native culture, nor that of his host country.

Rebecca, whose passion for humanitarian work and respect for all religions got her imprisoned, crossed the border into Cairo. Despite the lack of safety on the Cairene streets, and the terror of being isolated, she courageously holds on to her priorities, and sets goals for adaptation and service to the community.

Ibrahim, a student in his early twenties, is forced to leave his country to escape being persecuted by the Sudanese government. A staunch opponent of his government's discriminative laws, Ibrahim remains active in pursuing refugee interests.

Melissa traveled to Egypt while pregnant and with five children in tow to meet her husband, who had earlier fled from Sudan. While she struggles to make ends meet, she is able to provide her children with some education, and to establish a routine that keeps her family intact.

George, a well-educated man from a rich Christian family, who lived in southern Sudan, finds himself having to live and survive in the forest in order to escape being attacked by militant Islamists in his region. He eventually escaped to Egypt.

Urged by his mother to leave Burundi, **Nkosana** wrestles with his inability to feel emotion. The war has rendered everything senseless. Living in Cairo begins with hope, yet quickly becomes threatening, as his chances for survival become minimal.

Surviving a difficult birth, the struggling newborn acquires the nickname **Mahzouz**—meaning 'fortunate.' As the son of a warrior, Mahzouz struggles first with long periods of paternal absence and later with the turmoil of displacement.

After her father's death, **Mariette**, once affluent, becomes destitute. She married and moved to Cairo, where she uses her entrepreneurial talents to help raise her family's standard of living.

Ali, a 40-year-old father, is displaced from Kordofan in Sudan where he worked as an operations manager at the local airport. Suspected of smuggling medicine and food to the rebels in the south, Ali fled with his wife and children to the slums of Cairo.

Mishca, who comes from a high-profile family, chose to seek asylum in Cairo to study medicine. When her dreams of becoming a doctor are lost, she works her way through a degree in commerce, and works with teenagers to eliminate gang violence.

We present this book as a testament to the strength of its subjects.

The storywriters, the author of the Afterword, and one of the book's co-editors are students in the Rhetoric and Composition Department at the American University in Cairo. For a community-based service-learning project assigned by Amani Elshimi and Brooke Comer, who also serve as the manuscript's coeditors, students interviewed and collected the oral histories of a number of Sudanese refugees in order to raise awareness of their 'individuality.' As with all service-learning projects, this manuscript provides evidence that learning is most impassioned when it is invaluable to others.

As the writers worked with the storytellers, barriers of culture, education, and nationality were lowered, and friendships were formed. Three refugees—Bahja, Ali, and Farouq—have, since the writing of the stories, been relocated to the United States. Several student writers have graduated, become employed, or enrolled in graduate school. But the friendships continue.

"I have a story to tell. I am no hero. I am like you. I could be your brother, father, uncle, cousin. I could be you. In another time, in another place, this could be your story and that's why you must understand. I am one man, with one story, but there are many more like me."

—Ibrahim

Bahja

Nora Eltahawy
Mohamed Farag

It was 3am when they came. Our men, on their way to fagr prayer at the time, came running back in as the first bullets were fired. When it was over, my father, my uncle, and my father's cousins were among the dead, lying in the middle of our burning home.

We weren't surprised when they came. You could say . . . we were expecting them.

I was born in southern Darfur, in a town called Nyala, to a family of ten. My father, like the Fur tribe to which we belonged, had huge influence in the region. The only licensed dealer of foreign currency (or *kotkot* as we called it), his business was the reason behind our family's travels. Shortly after I was born, we moved to Jeneina—on the Sudan/Chad border—so my father could run his business. Even though I was a young girl at the time, I still remember the men President Nimeiri had sent to guard us on our journey from Jeneina to Marla, where we eventually settled, and where I spent most of my life.

In Marla, my father's business flourished, and my family lived on the nicest plantation in the village. Even though the irrigation system was primitive at the time, our gardens still grew mangos, guavas, lemons—the best fruit of every season. My father, who owned seven hundred cows, would always keep one for charity, and people in need would come to our barns and milk it for free. Our family also took in the village widows (women who were often without any source of income) and my father would bury the dead of families too poor to afford funerals.

When I was fourteen, our family gained a new member when I was married to a man twelve years my senior. I was still a student at the time, but following Sudanese custom, I dropped out of my studies and married as soon as I reached puberty. Two years later, and after I had given birth to the first of our many children, I went back to school and studied until I got my high school diploma. My husband, in the meantime, bought and sold *kotkot* with my father, and our household got bigger and bigger as my siblings wed and their spouses moved in.

Even though I couldn't continue to university (despite sitting the entrance test), I learned a great deal at the hands of an unexpected visitor, Mr. Rosanza. Part of a delegation sent by Italy to work on the railroads between Marla and Darfur, Rosanza had heard of the quality of the dairy products our family manufactured. Befriending my family, he and his Sudanese wife moved in with us for three years. My family loved the Italian and his wife, and my father and Rosanza set up a deal: in exchange for all the milk and cheese he could want, the Italian would send for machine parts from his homeland and improve our irrigation system. Besides his help with the irrigation, Rosanza left our family with one other important contribution—he taught my siblings and me English.

In 2003, as we listened to the Nyala radio, no one in my family assumed the trouble would reach us too, and that the reason behind our trouble would be the very plantation on which we lived. Instead, we just listened. We learned that, on Eid a nearby village was bombed; that, on another occasion, students sitting their exams were killed when their school was bombed in Teena; and that three days later, Darfur's airport was destroyed. As the location of the attacks got closer and closer to Marla, I grew more frightened at the prospect of us being attacked. I decided to talk to my father.

"I think you should sell the animals," I had said, "It's safer for us to move to another city."

"Never," my father had replied, "If we leave, who will take care of Marla's poor? Besides, it doesn't matter where we live. Death, my girl, follows you regardless of where you are."

As it turned out, I was not the only one who wanted my father to sell. A while after our conversation, my father received two guards sent by Nyala's *wali* in our home. Although he didn't know who the men were when they first arrived, my father delayed asking for the purpose of their visit. Instead, after being offered tea and a specially prepared meal, the men went to sleep, and it was only during the second day of their visit that they made their intentions clear:

"We were sent by Nyala's wali to make you an offer. He wishes to buy your plantation and is offering you 300,000,000 dinars for its purchase. Should we tell him you agree?"

"I'm sorry, but that's not possible," was my father's answer, "I can't sell what isn't mine. This land belongs to my children and has been in the family for generations. Tell the wali I turn his offer down."

And so the guards left. In the days following their visit, I worried that my father's refusal would bring repercussions, and tried my best to convince him to change his mind. As when I had first spoken to him about moving away from Marla, my father was adamant. The land would not be sold.

I don't know much about Sudanese politics, but I know that my father's refusal to sell the land was the reason that thirty days later the Janjaweed arrived in Marla. Ignoring other houses in our village, the Janjaweed attacked our house first; my father was the first man they killed. In the confusion that occurred in my house that night, and as the men grabbed hold of me, I was only distantly aware of my mother's voice.

"You can't do that to her! She's seven months pregnant!" She was screaming. It did no good, though, because they forced my mother silent.

I was raped five times that night.

I don't know how long the attack lasted, but the Janjaweed were thorough in their destruction. My husband had a little store out of which he'd sell sugar and wheat, little things villagers might need. The men stole everything in our shop and looted the entire village. After they set houses on fire, they stole my husband's car and drove off away from Marla.

Even though we couldn't find all of our family, we knew we had to escape immediately. And so the next day I set off, along with my mother, my children, and my nephew to Kalema, a place we'd been told had a displacement camp. Both my mother's legs had been broken and my nephew and I wrapped her legs in a makeshift bandage and placed her on the one donkey we had left. One of the soldiers she'd tried to stop from raping me had hit her with the end of his gun until her legs broke and she had lost consciousness. Ordinarily, the journey to Kalema would have taken a day but because of my mother's injury and because of mine (I had been bleeding since the rape), it took us a week to arrive.

Once we settled in the camp, things were momentarily better. The camp would swarm with aid workers in the mornings; foreign men and women who would treat us well and give us food. To make extra money, my sons fired bricks. Two days after our arrival, I sensed that I was in labor. Because I knew my body, I knew I had to try and reach a hospital to give birth. I have only one kidney, and so had delivered my other babies by C-section. We left the camp for Nyala, where I knew there was a hospital that could operate on me, but we were stopped on the outskirts by the police.

"You can't come in," we were told, "People from conflict areas aren't allowed into Nyala. You people just destroy everything."

And so we rested in a straw house, until we could find it in ourselves to walk back to Kalema. In the camp I gave birth to what I feared was a dead baby. A woman in the camp told me to breastfeed my son and to rub his chest with hot tea water. Because of her advice, my son started breathing properly three days later.

A while after we arrived, a new batch of women and children came in from a nearby town. Although we didn't see it happen, the families described to us the horrific way in which they had lost their families. We were told how, in that village, men's stomachs were sliced open and then stuffed with another corpse's head. They would go on fitting dead heads into dead stomachs until each group of four bodies formed a gruesome square. The Janjaweed had become creative.

As these events were occurring, the Sudanese government was not much help. The one time they sent relief workers to the camp was long after the attacks, and the workers arrived with meager supplies, hardly enough for all the displaced families. But the stinginess was not the biggest problem we faced because of the government. Soon after we settled in Kalema, a number of fights broke out, and the Sudanese government decided to send policemen to watch over the camp. The men did anything but protect us. Waiting until nightfall, and until the foreign aid workers had left, the men would storm the campsite and rape the women. No female was spared—neither I nor my mother (whose legs had still not healed) could escape. The police were brutal with anyone who protested. When a young man tried to ward them off of his mother, they beat him until one side of his body was paralyzed. When some women decided to complain to a Sudanese man working with a foreign aid agency, the police cut the man's ears off with scissors before killing him. Foreigners were not immune either; an American relief worker was beaten when she protested the rapes as well.

After witnessing the brutalities that took place in the camp, I decided to move my family out of Kalema as soon as possible. We put together the money my sons had earned working on the bricks, and were also forced to sell our donkey for the fare to travel to Khartoum. Outside the camp, we found and rode in a man's car to the capital. The journey, which took five days, ended with the driver warning us to stay outside the city. Darfurians, he said, were attacked there on a regular basis. And so, like in Nyala, we were forced to stay out of Khartoum—making camp, instead, in a slum area outside the city where many other displaced natives of Darfur were living.

My family and I lived in the slum area for several months and, during our stay, I took a job as a maid for a UN employee. I had been directed to the job by an aid worker who told me about a UN agency that hired Sudanese workers. Things went smoothly for two weeks, until we were abducted by government officials. Four plain-clothes policemen came to our house at night, grabbed me and my two eldest sons, and forced us into their car. After beating the boys and throwing them out of the vehicle, the men blindfolded me and I was driven to a house I'd never seen before. A man I mistakenly took to be kind asked me about my life. Even though I told him everything, he wrote nothing down, and a short while after he'd left me, another man came in and beat me until I threw up. I was locked in a room without food or water for an entire day, and only found out the reason behind my arrest the next day:

"You think that those foreigners are being kind to you, but they really only want to occupy Sudan. You are the reason. You are the fools of Darfur. You go and work with those foreigners, you go to those NGOs. You are a traitor."

It was the first man I had spoken to in the house.

I was stripped naked and beaten until they threw me back in the room I had been locked in. This time, it was for three days. When they finally checked in on me, I had not eaten or drunk anything for seventy-two hours and was scared for the condition of my one kidney. My captors denied my request for water. Instead, they told me they would only let me go if I promised to spy on the man whose house I cleaned. I was given CDs and discs so I could copy any information I found. I was told they would kill my children in front of me if I refused the mission.

After I was sent back, I told my children not to ask me where I was. When I finally retuned to work, and when my employer asked about my absence, I lied and said I had been sick with malaria. Eventually, I asked to speak to him about a private matter and asked for his help in leaving Sudan. I admitted I had lied about the malaria, but told him I needed to get out because of family and medical problems.

"I want to go to Egypt."

He had been surprised. "But why? I think it's better for you to go somewhere else. Kenya, maybe."

"No. I want to go to Egypt. It's an Arab and a Muslim country and that's where I choose to go."

Despite my employer's warnings, I was able to buy a black market passport and, a few months later, sailed to Aswan with my family.

Like the refugees who'd traveled with me, I knew that I had to find the UN office in Cairo right away. As luck would have it, one of the people I asked for directions, a Sudanese woman, offered to have my children and I stay at her home. I knew the woman was Christian, and it made me happy to see the war uniting us in this way. Before the crisis in Darfur, we were separated by class and religion. But now, outside our country's borders, we were all Sudanese.

Because the woman had to finish her day at work before taking us home, my family and I waited for her on the street, and it was on that sidewalk that I saw my husband again.

"You're hallucinating Bahja," I'd told myself, "your husband is dead."

But what I thought was a hallucination was running toward us, and then was hugging my children.

"Where have you been? I thought you were dead! How are you here?" The questions were many, and my husband's story was long.

In the mayhem that had occurred the night of the attack, I hadn't noticed that the Janjaweed had loaded my husband into our family car. One of the few men who survived, he was kept alive to be used as a driver. Tortured badly, my husband managed to escape from the hospital he had ended up in and, like us, had decided to escape to Egypt.

"I'm staying at a woman's apartment, I'm sure she wouldn't mind having you. . . ."

"Are you married to her?" I had interrupted. I couldn't help it.

"No! She takes in refugees, gives them food and money. That's all." And with that mind, and after apologizing to the woman I'd met earlier, we set off.

We settled into a sort of routine in Cairo. After getting my initial refugee card and US$100 from the UN, I took to the streets. I learned how to get around the city, where to go to get donations from churches and mosques, and I would constantly visit the UN office to try and learn what was to become of us.

It was on one of those trips to the UNHCR that I came across some Sudanese people sitting in the park of Mustafa Mahmoud Square.[4]

"Why are you here?" I'd asked.

"We're protesting," a man had answered me. "We're sick of the way we're being treated by the UN."

Once I learned that the people in the park had been sent back empty-handed and without hope by the UN as many times as I had been, I decided to join their sit-in along with my family.

We stayed in that little park for three months and, in that time, created an organized mini-society for ourselves. We had elected leaders and security men from among us, and they were responsible for maintaining order—no offense ever went unnoticed. Sometimes men who had disobeyed the group's policies would be hanged upside down from a tree as punishment. At night, men and women slept on separate sides of the garden, and we trekked to the nearby mosque anytime we needed to use the bathroom. When Ramadan came, we collected money from among ourselves for food. That's why we were so shocked when we heard the Egyptians accusing us of taking all the food from *mawa'id al-Rahman* (charity tables), of defecating in the park space, and of having sex out in the open.

The negotiations went on for a long time. I remember, at one point, we were told Adel Imam, acting as a goodwill ambassador for the UN, was willing to pay us each LE 300 to leave the garden. But we stayed. Women gave birth, people died, and we stayed. When it finally looked like the UN would agree to our terms, we learned that one of our requests—getting guarantees from the American, Australian, and Finnish embassies—would not be fulfilled, and the negotiations came to a stop.

Then, on the night of December 29 2005, everything changed.

The police started lining up in front of the garden at four in the afternoon. At the beginning, we were lied to. Talking to some of our men, the police warned them that a popular grass-roots movement in the country was making plans to attack and kill us all. Sensing it was a lie, we stayed on the grounds, and four hours later we saw the arrival of the Egyptian foreign minister along with even more armed guards.

"You have two hours to evacuate the park." The minister had yelled into a megaphone, "We've prepared places for you to stay."

Suspecting that this was another lie, and that the police merely wanted to load us onto ships back to Sudan, none of us moved, not even when several warning sirens were sounded.

And then the police changed tactics.

The freezing water came first. Blasting us with jets from powerful hoses, the police also released a gas into the grounds that made me drowsy. Confused and disoriented, I was only vaguely aware of a woman near me who was being beaten so hard I could see her intestines peeking out of her skin. I saw another mother, running with her baby, fall on one of the garden's sharp fences. They were both staked to death. And then I was being dragged, felt my breasts being pulled at, and thrown into a bus. I saw a naked woman with a bleeding head being thrown into the bus after me. Knowing that she couldn't possibly be alive, my fellow passengers and I covered her. None of my family members were on the bus with me. I was sure I'd lost them forever.

It was a long drive to the prison on the Alexandria Desert Road and, on the way, several more passengers on my bus died. The hardest part of the ordeal for me was when we were finally let off the bus, and I found one of my sons in the crowd, crying. I didn't have time to look for any of my other children, before I was pushed into my cell, but I knew that they had scattered us among several prisons in Egypt.

It shouldn't have come as a surprise that we were treated badly by the prison guards. One day, a guard came into our cell and raped a twenty-two-year-old Sudanese girl. I remember the people pleading with him that day to spare the poor girl, but nothing worked. On another occasion, prison doctors came in to give injections they described as painkillers. I don't know what was in them, but I saw people collapsing after they were injected; I saw one woman lose bits of her skin as well.

It was only on the fifth day of imprisonment that we were loaded onto buses that took us around the other prisons so we could look for our families. I was told that my husband was tortured and that some of my children had already been released, and one by one I tried to reunite with those still in jail. I remember it was very difficult finding one of my sons. I learned afterward that, mistaken for dead after the attack on the *midan* garden, he had been put in the mortuary with dead bodies. By the time we were forced to stop looking, I still couldn't find one of my daughters or my nephew.

By that time, news of what had happened to us had reached the NGOs and they started coming to see us in prison, bringing food and medicine. I recognized one of the UN men sent to the prison and when I ran to introduce myself, I found that he remembered me too. It was through this man's help that my family members and I were finally released from prison a few days later.

On the outside, the only event that brought me happiness was receiving a phone call from a Sudanese woman who had found and had been taking care of my daughter.

To this day, I cannot find my nephew.

I wish that the suffering was limited to the attacks on the square, at Mustafa Mahmoud, or its aftermath, but we suffer every day. Before my imprisonment, I was working in a nearby hospital. These days, cleaning jobs are the only ones I can get. Egyptian schools won't accept my children, so we're forced to send them to a private one whose fees we can't afford. Donations from churches and NGOs are getting smaller and smaller, and the only way we can live is through the generosity of people.

In addition to money, our biggest problem in this country is harassment. Besides the daily maltreatment we suffer no matter where we go, I was also attacked and robbed by four men as I was coming out of the metro one day. I lost all my UN papers. Another time, I was thrown out of a hospital I had gone to to get my kidney checked, because of no fault of my own. The trouble had started when patients in the waiting room with me had started verbally abusing the Sudanese.

"But aren't we all Arabs and Muslims? Don't we all live in a Muslim country?" I had asked one of them. I should've anticipated their reply.

"No we are not the same. You're black and I'm white and you should get out of our country."

Ihsan

Malak El Khadem
Menna Shafei

When I was a child, I used to love the color white because I thought it represented hope, peace, and the future. Then, there came a time when I stopped believing in those things. My name is Ihsan Abd Rabou. I am 33 years old, and I grew up in the northern part of Darfur in Sudan. My father died when I was young, so I grew up with my younger sister, our mother, and grandmother. We are, like most Darfurians, a Muslim family.

My sister Roqaya and I used to sleep in one of the two rooms that composed our small, humble house, the kind of house that you only have to glance at to know its residents are very poor. But I liked my house, because it symbolized safety and warmth for me. I liked it because it was my own. What I was too young to realize was that it was not all that safe for four women to live on their own. But, we managed to forge close relationships with our neighbors who treated us like we were part of their family too. And it was these bonds that gave us strength and safety—that saved us from being women on their own.

When I was six years old, I went to a small school in our neighborhood. It was a poor government school that had no real resources or books, but I loved it because it gave me a chance to meet my friends. Unfortunately, my experience at the school didn't last long. Since my mother could not afford the fees, my sister and I only stayed long enough to learn to read and write. We were still quite young when our formal education ended but we did not stop learning. We stayed home to bake bread with my mother and the women in our neighborhood. It was such a pleasant time that I still remember it with joy and nostalgia and, not surprisingly, cooking became my favorite hobby.

17

This childhood gathering of women in the kitchen also inspired me to learn to sing, perhaps because there was always music in the air. All my female relatives and family friends used to sing and hum while they sat together, and no one was lazy. If they weren't baking, they were always busy doing some-thing; my grandmother was either reading fortunes in coffee cups and telling a cousin or niece whom they would marry, or she was braiding an aunt's or a close friend's hair. These were my grandmother's two special talents and she taught them both to me. They would serve me well later, though I did not know it at that time.

The art of reading fortunes is usually passed on from mother to daugh-ter, but my mother did not have this gift, and so I learned from my grand-mother. I would watch her as she carefully prepared a cup of coffee for her client, who would then drink it. When all the liquid had been consumed, the way the grounds were arranged told my grandmother a great deal about the woman's life. The clients were always women and most of them wanted to know who they would marry or, if they were already married, whether their husband was cheating on them. I should not call them clients, because my grandmother never took money from them. Though, later in my life, I would be able to supplement my meager income by reading fortunes. My grandmother shared her gift generously; she did it for the pure pleasure of helping people. She gave the names of loved ones, hated ones, she could predict success and failure in love, business and education. I remember that she never said anything about death. She used to say that only God could predict death. After my grandmother had finished giving a reading, I would ask her how she could know so much about a person by looking at the coffee grounds in their cup. She never gave me a clear answer, perhaps because there isn't one. Perhaps it is something felt, and not known, an instinct or a kind of magic. I think that this is not so much a skill that can be learned, but a gift, and I consider myself lucky to have inherited her talent.

Hairdressing, namely braiding hair into tiny strands known as 'cornrows,' was another one of my grandmother's special talents that she passed down to me. Although it sounds easy, it requires dexterity. You begin to tie the hair together at the root, and then knot it a little more loosely down the neck. It takes a long time to finish and in some countries, braiding is quite expensive. Women like it because it keeps their hair in place for as long as three or four months without any effort at all.

I was sorry that I had to stop going to school but what I learned in the kitchen, in the company of women, were the trades that would keep me alive when I moved to a new country much later on. In addition, no matter how much danger rumbled outside our door, no matter how unstable Darfur became, I will never forget the feeling of safety and security that I found in the kitchen. Needless to say, that didn't last for a long time. The recurrent tension in our neighborhood was escalating every day, as we used to hear about an increasing number of deaths and serious injuries. Every day, someone that we knew was killed.

Before I quit going to school, I would walk the short distance to class from my house. It was not uncommon to find a dead body in a corner of the street in the early morning light. The first time I stumbled upon a body was a horrible moment in my life; I felt sickened, and ran quickly the rest of the way to school. Later, the image of this dead body haunted me. I left school and ran home crying. When I told my mother about what I had seen, she tried to calm me down. But it was clear that she too was upset, not only by my tears but because of the state of violence that had erupted in Darfur. My sister was also a reluctant witness to murder victims, as many people were killed at that time in random massacres. But we were lucky; there were far more horrible fates awaiting young girls than having to step over a dead body on the street. Many girls were raped, in fact, and every three or four days we'd hear about a girl we knew who had been the victim of a sexual attack.

As the violence increased, the economy became worse; there were fewer and fewer jobs and no one had enough money. We were managing our lives day-by-day, but we could not continue without a clue about whether we would have enough money to eat the next day. My mother decided that my sister and I should leave Sudan and look for a better life in Egypt. We'd heard stories from neighbors with family members who had found work there, could make a living, and who felt safe. My mother could not go with us because my grandmother was too old to be left alone or to travel, so we found neighbors who agreed to travel with us, for our safety. They had friends in Cairo who, they promised, could help us find jobs.

In Cairo, a city that overwhelmed me with its color and noise, our neighbors directed us to the house of a Sudanese family who had also moved from Darfur. They were living in Arba Wa Nus,[5] a very poor area in Cairo, with dirt streets lined with small shops selling mobile phones and bread, two staples. In Arba Wa Nus, many of the apartments do not have electricity or running water and as many as ten to twenty people sleep in each small one-room apartment, which can be rented for as little as US$15 a month. African refugees and poor Egyptians share this neighborhood, but living together in common poverty does not make them close. There is a kind of tension between them, an invisible barrier. We were taken to a home that was very small, poor, and dirty. There was no floor, but hard-packed dirt under our feet. The entire building of residents shared one squalid bathroom. This was my introduction to Cairo.

Cairo may not seem like an expensive city to someone from the western world, but to my sister and me, it was a costly place to live. I knew that I needed to make money quickly and I soon realized there was a market for my two talents. I relied on my skills as a hairdresser and a fortuneteller to sustain us. Most of the women who wanted their hair braided were also refugees on limited budgets, so I could not make a great deal of money from this kind of work. But I used my talent as a fortuneteller to survive when I first arrived in Cairo. I think that I took my gift further than my grandmother did because I became able to name a woman's future husband or identify the kind of danger that a particular challenge might lead to.

I built my client base by getting the word out through my friends. They worked as maids and would tell their employers, who were mainly upper-class women, about my fortunetelling abilities. This group, I have found, is often very interested in knowing what is going to happen to them in the future. They want to know who they will marry and what they need to watch out for. If they are married they want to know whether their husbands are telling the truth when they say they are on a business trip, or if they are off at a beach resort with a pretty secretary. I was soon able to make enough money to survive—to eat and pay rent. Demand for my skills increased, and soon I was being hired to read coffee cups for large groups of women at parties or special events. I grew to enjoy it. I like sitting in a circle with these women, whose faces hold so much expectation as they wait to hear what I am going to tell them. Perhaps it reminds me of my childhood days in the kitchen. I always feel safe and secure in the company of women.

Reading fortunes was something I enjoyed, but the work was not consistent. Once women have their fortunes read, they don't need another reading for many months, maybe even a year. So I took a job as a live-in maid for a family; I cooked, cleaned, and took care of their house. Because I slept in a small room in the family house, I was always 'on call,' and obliged to be available anytime and to do anything asked of me. I did not have time to rest or to even see my sister. I worked all day and sometimes late into the night. It was in this house that a most shameful incident occurred to me. I was 27 years old and the family I worked for had a 21-year-old son who used to tease me and flirt with me in an inappropriate way. I could not tell him to stop and I was afraid of telling my Madame for fear that she might not believe me, or that she might even kick me out before I had been paid. I had no one to talk to about this problem and silenced by my desperate need for money and food, I became deeply frustrated. My sister still did not have a job, so I was responsible for both of us. And for some reason, the family I worked for would not allow my sister to come and visit me in their house, which made me realize that this was a bad situation, an employer I did not want to work for. But what choice did I have? Then one day a terrible thing occurred. My Madame's son went too far with his flirting and touching and he had his way with me against my will. I was so upset and ashamed that I left their house without telling anyone or even taking my monthly salary.

I did not think I could ever work in someone's house again, which made things difficult because what other opportunities did I have to find food, lodging, and a salary? My sister got a job as a hairdresser in a salon, braiding hair and drawing henna tattoos, but she did not continue. She faced many instances of humiliation, ill-treatment, and harassment by her employers, and the salary was not enough. The salon where she worked was far away from home and she could barely scrape together the extra money she needed just to be able to get to work every day. Then her luck changed; one of her regular customers asked her to be a live-in nanny for le 500 per month (about US$90). My sister told me about this salary and I was shocked, as I had only been making le 350. I had no idea that people in Egypt would pay such a high salary. My sister started her new job as a nanny, and the family she worked for was good to her and she was very happy. Soon after, her employer asked her if she had any friends or relatives who could work as a nanny for her sister, also for le 500 a month. This is how I found the beloved family I work for now. They are such kind people, and for the past four and a half years they have treated me with respect.

One of our family friends from Darfur, who traveled with us to Cairo, was a young man named Ismail. Once in Cairo, Ismail found a good job as a driver. In my new career as a nanny, when I finally had stability and dignity, I realized that I was in love with Ismail and he let me know that the feeling was mutual. We got married, and we now live in a small house with my sister. We still have our jobs, which take us out of the house much of the time, but it is good to have a place to call home, that is our own, and with a kitchen that is warm and friendly.

Ismail and I are saving to have a baby. This is one thing we both agree on: It is important to save for the future. In my spare time, I use my special talents—hairdressing, fortunetelling, baking special breads and cakes, and doing henna tattooing—to make a little extra money. My extra income also allows me to afford my life in Cairo and to have a few tiny luxuries, like new dresses. But best of all, I am happy. My sister says that working in a house with people who have known you for a long time and who like you is safe and secure, and she is right. Being in a kitchen gives me the same feeling of comfort I had as a child, baking and singing while the horrors of Darfur raged just outside the door.

Today, I am able to use the skills I learned in childhood to supplement my salary and save up for my future child. I earn LE 10 for each coffee cup I read, which is not much alone, but I usually give readings in groups, for four or five people in a row. I also bake bread and sell it in the area where I live, to African, and even Egyptian women, because they like it. I sell five loaves for LE 5. I continue to braid hair for my friends, but I do not take money for this. I don't think it is right to take money for doing someone a favor. And I still love the color white. It is the color of peace and hope. It represents my future, with all the mysteries and wonders that I know it holds.

Joseph

Ahmed Khalifa

To be frank, I can't say that my childhood was a bad one. I grew up with many friends, a caring and concerned family, and most of all, I had a life free of troubles and conflict. That isn't to say that I didn't come across troubles or difficult predicaments later in my life. All I am trying to say is that the time I spent growing up in Khartoum during my adolescent years before high school was pleasant, and the time after high school was the most agonizing. But it was also the most memorable time of my life, because agony is hard to forget. I believe that from the point at which I discovered agony, from that point onward, my life began to change drastically.

I'm sorry. I have been confiding in you and I haven't even introduced myself yet. My name is Joseph and I am part of the Dinka tribe of southern Sudan. To be more specific, my family originates from Dinka Yirol, the village of my father. My mother is from Dinka Bor, a close province next to Yirol. In our culture, it is a customary when one asks you where you are from to reply with the name of your father's hometown. That is why Yirol is officially my hometown, despite the fact that I have never seen it or even come close to it. One might think that everyone who comes from Yirol is destined to become a doctor. My father is a doctor as are two of my brothers. Perhaps it runs in the family. But I never lived in Yirol because I was born in Khartoum in 1970. When I look back and think of those numbers in my head, it seems as if I'm already old.

The years growing up in Khartoum were some of the best in my life. I was keen to go to school and I was a good student. I wasn't a slow child, the kind who would remain confused and lost throughout the lesson, nor was I one of those spoiled boys who would cut class or avoid work whenever they got the chance. No, I was dedicated and I was interested in making the most of myself. Maybe that had something to do with my father. His father wasn't a rich man, but we were a moderately well-off family. His profession gave us a good life and provided us with the necessities.

My father was stern, however, and always busy. He was a high-level health official responsible for deciding what medications were allowed to enter the Sudanese market. Due to the extreme demands of his job, he was rarely at home. Despite these absences, it was he who shaped my thoughts and opinions. I remember him being rigid, not a man to laugh easily, to humor his children, or to take matters lightly. But, despite being reserved, he was fair and humble. Regretfully, I never knew much about his work. Medicine never really interested me but I grew to respect his patience, fairness, self-control, and—most of all—his selflessness. He rarely favored his sons over his daughters, which was admirable at that time, admirable in Sudan at any time. It was through our night-long debates that I came to see his true colors and learn the principles and values he believed in.

All the nurturing and tenderness I missed in my father, I found in the rich and full character of my mother. She was caring, loving, concerned, and—most of all—selfless. I admire the time, energy, and patience she devoted to her nine children, even though, by Sudanese standards, this was a small or an average-sized family. Other than my love for my parents, I don't remember much about growing up in Khartoum. That may be due to the fact that my childhood was painless and free from any sort of torment or painful encounter. Perhaps happy memories often fade away faster, while painful or agonizing moments are ingrained into your life.

While growing up in Khartoum I remained detached from the friction that was intensifying in the south, as it simply did not concern me or my loved ones. When my father asked me what job I was interested in, he hoped that I would study medicine and follow in his footsteps. But I had no interest in that. I thought three physicians were enough for one family. It wasn't my destiny. From as far back as I can remember I was always a passionate writer. Whenever I was in a state of frustration or anger or mere boredom, I found that I could always vent my emotions through writing and the power that accompanies it. This passion, eventually, started to cause me many problems.

Not everyone understands the intricacies of Sudan's political history or the events and people that have shaped the country to become what it is now. The essence of Sudan's conflict has its roots in Sudanese tribal history. I was born in 1970, at that time Gaafar Nimeiri was still president of Sudan. During Nimeiri's time in office there was little conflict between the south and the north. Many remember this decade as one of peace and sovereignty. Although Nimeiri was yet another leader who had assumed his presidential position through a military coup, during his term the economy was stable, the people were well-off, and—most of all—war was not waged in every province of the south.

Many remember Nimeiri as one who did not discriminate according to religion or ethnicity. I remember that during his time the government paid for education and therefore all universities and schools were accessible.

Today, when I come across a fellow Sudanese of my generation and we reminisce about the past, most agree that Gaafar Nimeiri was by far the most decent and merciful of all presidents of Sudan. When I say "most" agree with me, but I mean everyone except for my father. He believed that Nimeiri was oppressive and tyrannical because he assumed power through a military coup. Because my father is a fair and just man, he could never understand how anyone could assume a leadership position by force. He felt that force was never the solution, and that a leader could only rule well after obtaining the consent and approval of the people. When Omar Bashir assumed office in the summer of 1989, most informed Sudanese knew that a new period of change was in store, and one that would make a serious impact on the country. What kind of impact it would make? Who could then say?

After he took office, I had plenty to say about the influence of President Bashir's regime on Sudan. During his first term, I was still in school—an energetic, dedicated, and bright student, I am proud to say. As a student, I learned to develop my writing skills through practice and by reading literature. I joined the school newspaper *Africa News* and soon became a writer, expressing my most intimate and ambitious goals to the school. I also became the chief editor of the "African Culture" section and was allowed once a week to convey my opinion in the "Politics" section. I soon began to write about the appalling conditions my country faced, giving much blame to the current regime, and the inadequate implementation of certain policies concerning education, freedom of expression, and the Sudanese constitution with regard to equal rights and opportunities. Before I knew it, I found myself writing solely in the politics section, becoming more and more passionate about social change, and more aggravated by the lack of justice and democracy. What I didn't know was the kind of trouble my articles would get me into. I had no idea that my high school newspaper journalism would change and traumatize my life.

It was the first day of the holy month of Ramadan and it was late at night. I had been staying late at school to help with the weekly issue, which would go to print the next day. After I finished my work, I left school with a friend and we walked home. A car pulled over suddenly, several men seized us, jammed us into the car, and drove off. I was blindfolded and told to shut up if I wanted to see another day. My hands were tied and I was placed in a constrained position. I shall never forget the discomfort and fear I felt at that moment.

How long the drive was, I cannot tell. I didn't know who had kidnapped us or what they wanted. Though blindfolded and overcome with fear, I knew we weren't going very far. Had we been heading far off, then the road would be straight. Our drive was bumpy and took a lot of curves, indicating that we were still in the city, and that the frequent turns were simply to confuse us into thinking that we were going somewhere far out of anyone's reach. When the car doors finally opened, someone seized my arm, yanked me out of the car, and told me to walk. I was pushed into a cell, with a cold floor that almost paralyzed me the first night. I don't know which emotion is stronger—fear or confusion. I was incredibly scared for my life. I did not know if I would see my family again. Would I be tortured? Would I be killed, and would no one ever learn what had happened to me? What had I done? Could my articles be taken so seriously? The following morning I was to find the answers to all these questions.

I woke up to the sound of a man being beaten, a man whose strength I could never have imagined. The beatings would not stop, yet he persisted. Eventually, it was my turn. My captors would punch me until I fell over, kick me while I was on the ground, and use any means to inflict pain upon me. I never felt so helpless, so humiliated, or so vulnerable to the actions of another. I tried to remain strong, but it is just overwhelming how much pain one human can inflict on another. When several men kicked me, I would curl up into a ball with my arms wrapped around my head and my knees pressed against my chest. I did this to protect my most vulnerable organs from damage. Curling myself into a ball made my back more susceptible to kicks. If they found that my head was protected and my stomach was blocked from a free blow, then the only place which they were free to kick and punch as they liked was my back. As a result, my spinal cord has suffered greatly.

The daily beatings were not the only method of torture that I had to bear. Often, I would be taken to another room for interrogation. Whenever I left my cell, I would be once again blindfolded so that my interrogator's identity would be protected. I hated these interrogations, sometimes even more so then the beatings. They would ask me whether I was "pro-American," or whether I was opposed to Omar Bashir's government.

I could never remember what I said in response. I may have remained silent or, perhaps, have said anything just to stop the beatings and the dunking of my head into water. To a certain degree, I was a difficult prisoner, for I remained silent a lot of the time. I remember once, they were so frustrated with my lack of cooperation that they took me to witness another man being tortured. Two men held the captive and a third ripped every single nail off of his fingers with a pair of metal pincers. I trembled uncontrollably. Once again, they placed me in my cell and the usual four thugs entered the cell without saying a word. They did not need to. I knew they were there to 'knock' some sense into me. After the second week, I was told to sign a document. I tried reading but it was snatched from my hands and I was told I had no right to read; I had only to sign. They would release me, I was promised, if I chose to cooperate. Suddenly, I decided to comply with their requirements. I wanted freedom, I wanted to see my family, and I wanted to get my life back. I signed the document without reading it and was taken back to my cell. I got two more routine beatings, was blindfolded, dumped in a car, and driven around in circles and then eventually released. I had been in prison for two weeks.

I can't even begin to tell you how relieved and grateful I was to step into my house. As my family wept and pleaded, I had to promise I would stop writing about political issues, altogether. This was what interested me most in the world, yet I had to give it up. I had to accept and respect my mother's plea. And, I didn't want to go through hell again.

Life resumed yet seemed to lose its color. I saw everything in gray and I had a vague paranoia that someone was watching me, observing my every step and action. I worried, though I wasn't doing anything wrong. People at *Africa News* asked me questions. I simply shrugged and said that I had family issues.

Before I knew it, I had graduated from high school and was considered a man, someone self-sufficient and independent. It was in 1990, and at that time I met a girl named Ann. She was cute, shy, loving, and affectionate in every way. I grew very fond of her and decided I must marry her. In Sudan, it is a custom to seek the consent and approval of both parents. Her parents agreed; mine did not. I was furious. My father explained that although she, like me, came from the Dinka tribe, Ann's tribe came from a sub-province where the women are considered to be "promiscuous" and "loose." I asked how my father could pass such a judgment when he had never even met her, or spoken to her. How could he, who was presumably so just and fair, come up with such an unsound conclusion? But the decision was final: I would not be marrying Ann. Eventually, Ann's parents heard about my father's reaction, and withdrew their approval too. Until this very day, every love experience in my life continues to be associated with complications. I have thus learned to concentrate on the more concrete aspects of life: a job, a permanent place of residence, and a secure place back in my homeland.

When I finished high school, my father sent me to study abroad. I was accepted at the University of Alexandria in Egypt, and I moved there in the summer of 1991. Alexandria, back then, was a small, clean, beautiful city. I decided to study Arabic literature. I knew I would excel and develop my writing potential to its fullest. I made many friends and grew to love Egypt, a great deal more than I do today.

During my holiday, I decided to visit my uncle in Juba, in the central southern part of Sudan, a place which is isolated and dangerous if you don't know your way around. My uncle, who is an army general, offered to host me in his house, which would be safe from all the crime and shootings that occurred outside the compounds. Because I was not known in that area, I would be much more vulnerable to theft or arrest. I made sure that I never left my uncle's house unaccompanied.

One night, while I was fast asleep, the SPLA (Sudanese People's Liberation Army) snuck into a military base and killed 150 officers or more as they slept. They fled immediately, unseen and unheard by anyone. The only evidence that they were ever present was the bodies of 150 officers, who had been brutally stabbed to death. When this happened, my uncle woke me up and informed me that I was caught up in a great mess. As I did not belong to that provincial area, I could be a potential suspect in the crime. The airport and military compound nearby were closed so that no one would be able to enter or leave the crime scene. My uncle had to do a lot of explaining as to why I was coincidentally visiting the compound when the murders happened.

Shortly after that my uncle arranged for me to fly to Khartoum, where I would be safe and distant from the harassment in Juba. The airport was closed and the only flight going to Khartoum was a military plane transporting important officials away from harm should the SPLA strike again. My uncle had arranged for me to stay at his wife's family's house in Khartoum. I was unaware that a huge commotion was caused because of my presence in Juba.

I was escorted by a soldier to the house of my uncle's wife, who had to verify that I was his nephew. I stayed in that house for two months, during which I was not allowed to leave. The only place I could visit was the Army Club, situated nearby.

One night, at 3am, my brother, who was a police officer, told me to follow him to the Army Club and then to accompany him to the airport where he would finish some errands. I agreed wholeheartedly, as I had been locked up for two months and was happy to see any change in my daily surroundings. When we arrived at the airport, my brother told me to follow him. I was able to cross all security checks even though I was not flying anywhere. It was not until I passed the last gate that my brother told me, "I arranged your flight back to Cairo yesterday. Your passport is with that man over there. Now go and don't come back." Those were his last words and suddenly, in less than half an hour, I found myself aboard a plane that was already airborne. I arrived in the morning with nothing other than my passport. No luggage, no money, and no clue as to how I would survive in Egypt without any help.

I resumed my studies in Alexandria, but a year later, the situation in Sudan got worse. The Four Agreements which were signed by both Egypt and Sudan, and which funded my tuition fees, were broken and consequently I had to stop my education two years short of obtaining a degree. I was disappointed but mostly angry that something so distant could affect the way I wanted to live and achieve my goals. I forced myself to make the best of a bad situation and I began looking for employment, something or anything, to make ends meet.

In 1994, I got a job in Sharm al-Sheikh working in a diving club, where I met tourists of all kinds. The Italians were the most prominent nationality. They were such friendly people but somehow unsympathetic. I cannot complain about Italian women, though. They're a part of heaven. The only problem is that they always wanted to speak their own language and that often irritated me. Overall, my job was good. I was the only Sudanese worker there and I always felt that the hotel manager gave me special treatment. One day, I asked him, "Why are you so fond of Sudanese people?" He said, "I like you people because you are nice, truthful, and above all, you have endured a lot as a nation." I was grateful, yet didn't understand why he gave me a salary that was higher than other local workers' salaries. His explanation was that I needed it because of "family back home" and that "providing them with money is a necessity."

Whenever my Egyptian colleagues asked how much I make a month, I would simply ignore their question or reply that I make just as much as they do. One day a fellow Sudanese colleague told me to go to my room to see what had happened. I dashed upstairs to find that my belongings had been searched, and that the drawers and closets had been opened. I confronted Khaled, the security guard. He confessed that it was indeed he who was responsible for wrecking the room, but that he was following orders from above. I was infuriated and, in the heat of the moment, quit my job and returned to Cairo. Ever since then I have held a series of low-paying jobs. I have never really enjoyed any of my jobs the way I would have enjoyed being a journalist or an author. It's a situation I have to deal with and learn from.

My greatest hope is that I will marry a beautiful and vibrant girl that I have met on the Internet. I know what you're thinking—how can love work its magic in cyberspace? She is phenomenal. This summer I hope to meet her. She comes from a Spanish island in the Caribbean and her customs are different from mine. Yet this time I have faith that it shall work out somehow and that we can be together. I am learning Spanish at the moment so that when I propose to her, I can do it in her native tongue. I shall tell my mother and father and hope they understand that I am a grown man able to make the decision of whom to marry on my own. All I want is to start life afresh and see it through different eyes.

During these eight years in Cairo nothing has changed. Everything stays the same, except that the Egyptian people become less tolerant of my people.

Maybe that has something to do with their own struggles for a decent life. Life in Cairo seems to be a merry-go-round—color and noise and riches that only a few are able to grasp. The rest of us watch it all go by. What I want most of all is to go home, with my Caribbean bride, to see my mother and father again. I want to bury my feet in Sudanese soil and experience that feeling of being in my homeland. To live your life in exile is the most horrible thing in the world.

Farouq

Youssef Atwan
Nahla Mahgoub

3:14am. I just can't seem to fall asleep. The anticipation is draining. The pictures I saw earlier today of California neighborhoods, and the house that will be my home, are ingrained in my head. I'm excited but the questions on my mind are endless: What is life going to be like? Is it going to be easy to make friends? Will I be able to continue my education? Will we be able to support ourselves?

Like so many times in my life, I can't believe this is really happening. By this time tomorrow, my family and I will be on a plane headed for the United States. I keep picturing my mother's and my sisters' happy faces, hopeful for the first time in years. This time it's different. This time we're moving for one last time. This time, our life-long journey might actually be over!

I was only six years old when my parents decided to move to Egypt. Although I was young, I can vividly remember what I was feeling when I first arrived in Cairo. It was 1992, the year Cairo was shaken by a huge earthquake, and I remember the shock and the chaos it left behind. I also remember being frightened of the enormity of the Egyptian capital city, in comparison to the neighborhood I was born and raised in—Jeddah, Saudi Arabia. I remember standing timidly on a busy street, feeling lost in the huge city and amidst the massive number of people walking by. I asked my mother a million questions. Why did we leave our home? Why did we come to this scary place? Where were we going to live? At six years old, I didn't realize my mother had just as many questions as I did.

3:36am. I'm still wide awake. I look out my window and listen to the stillness outside. I've been living in Egypt for fourteen years now and I still feel like a stranger. My friends and memories are in Egypt, but I am yet to feel that I can call it home. Tonight's silence reminds me of Aziziya, my old neighborhood in Saudi Arabia. I recall hearing stories about how my father fled to the Kingdom after being chased by Sudanese police. He was a member of a political movement called the *Komolo* at the time and, like many of his contemporaries who joined anti-government organizations, he was forced to leave Sudan. My father reached Saudi Arabia through Yemen in 1982. It was in Saudi that my father married my mother, and it was also there that my siblings and I were born. Our father settled into his job at a publishing house and, for a while, our family was comfortable. Then my father took a trip to Sudan ... and never came back.

Sometimes I feel cursed to be Sudanese, war chasing me and my family everywhere we go, depriving us of any chance of a happy and peaceful life. Wasn't it war that made my father flee for his life from his own country? Wasn't it war —this time in the Gulf—that made it impossible for us to live our lives in Saudi Arabia, the place I was born? My mother has always told me stories about how things got worse for us after the Gulf War, how terribly foreigners were treated during the war and how my brother and I were not allowed to go to school just because we were Sudanese.

My mother is the strongest woman I have ever met. Throughout the harsh conditions that we've encountered, she has always been the person that everyone in the family leaned on. After things became intolerable in Saudi Arabia, she stood strong beside my father and decided to help him, and us, adjust to the new circumstances. Sudanese women are almost fanatical about supporting their families, and my mother is the living example. She's almost always happy, but losing yet another member of the family affected her terribly.

Right before we moved to Egypt in 1991, my mother received a letter from her ailing father asking her to visit Sudan to see him one last time. Naturally, my mother immediately set off, taking her eldest son—my brother Ibrahim—with her for company. As soon as my mother and brother reached a friend's house in Khartoum, the Sudanese police stormed into the house and arrested them both. The police, who sent them to 'Cuba'—an infamous prison in the country—told her she was being arrested because she was married to a political activist who was a wanted man. My brother and my mother were separated in the prison. It was the last time she saw him alive.

Nine days after their arrest, my brother died in the prison hospital; he had been tortured to death.

When I learned about my brother's death, I realized the world was an unreasonable and unjust place. That being a refugee means you are allowed only to suffer, and no questions are to be asked.

4:02am. It's a matter of hours before the flight takes off. I hate the wait—it reminds me of the times we waited in vain to be helped by refugee organizations. Our experience with the UNHCR started when we first applied for resettlement, back in 1992. In those days, it took five months for a refugee to get a meeting with the UNHCR office, and another two months before actually meeting with an officer. The first time we were interviewed we had faith we'd get our lives back, but when we were rejected refugee status and it took two more years to arrange a second interview, we knew better than to hope.

By the time my mother was called in for a second interview, our family was gripped by pessimism. I remember my mother telling us she felt she was being made to beg for something—for anything—inside the UNHCR office. I'll always feel angry when I remember the way my mother was treated inside those offices and I'll always resent the officer who showed her no respect. It's difficult for me to understand why an employee would treat a perfect stranger in such a horrible manner. Why would she take away our chances? There are a lot of unanswered questions in my mind. I can't seem to explain the neglect and the abuse of power by people in authority. Why is it directed at us? Why refugees?

Through six long years of rejection, all my mother and I could do was to keep struggling and hoping. We decided we wouldn't give up until we claimed our right to a decent life. In 2000, after another long series of appointments and interviews, our biggest fear came true: our case was permanently closed.[6] I knew it. Justice, dreams, hopes, and human rights were theories and fictional rights that only existed in books. Looking for protection and sanction is a farce. I realized that all efforts go astray if you are discriminated against or if you are treated only as a 'case' or a 'file' and not a living human being.

With our new 'closed file' status we had only two dreadful options: continue living in Egypt or go back to Sudan. Two options that felt equally deadly. The UNHCR advised us to go back to Sudan, asserting that peace was maintained in the south. The problem is that I had never been to Sudan and neither had my sisters. My mother had not set foot in Sudan since my brother died and most importantly, we are not even originally from the south! Could the UNHCR be any more ignorant and inconsiderate? We were nothing more than a bunch of names and numbers on some paper.

What the UNHCR did to us was no different to what the Egyptian police forces did to the Sudanese refugees camped in a small park, across the street, protesting to claim their rights. Those refugees had, like us, come to Egypt seeking asylum from persecution. What were they being beaten and punished for? And the Sudanese had always thought of Egypt as a second home and Egyptians as true brothers!

Outside the garden, during the protests, I was just another Sudanese troublemaker. But inside the garden, among my countrymen, my history as a child raised in Egypt meant I was perceived as an Egyptian. I could relate to neither side; neither side could relate to me. Ever since, the issue has been on my mind. I don't feel Egyptian, and I never did. On the other hand, I have never been to Sudan, I do not have many Sudanese friends, and I have never been exposed to the culture . . . all of which doesn't make me very Sudanese.

After what happened with the sit-in,[7] my mother's determination to get us out of the country grew even stronger. We had no life in Cairo. She went to the UNHCR again. My mother waited in front of the UNHCR offices day after day. My mother repeatedly told us that she did not have anything to lose and that she did not have any other options. She waited every day for the head of UNHCR to finish work and tried to get his attention as he was on his way to his car. Day after day, the security guards pushed her away. Day after day, she went again. Finally, after almost six months of waiting, the head of UNHCR asked why my mother was always waiting in front of their offices. Her sincerity and honesty that day convinced the man to take another look at her case and, miraculously, our case was reopened.

The alarm rings. I must have fallen asleep after all. I still feel exhausted from staying up late and from all the thinking. I could use some more sleep, but no! Today is my big day! I have been waiting fourteen long years for this day. Finally, today I'm traveling. I'm going to the new world, my new world. I'm finally granted a chance to live and to see my family live. Today, I'm headed for the United States where I have been granted the right of resettlement. Although I have a million worries and a million doubts, I realize I have come a long way, and I know in my heart that I deserve this chance.

As I sit on the plane, looking out the window, I can see how my life and my family's has been nothing but a cycle of hatred and prejudice. Like all refugees around the world, we have been discriminated against on the basis of our status. The world doesn't care about our dreams, hopes, and aspirations, and it doesn't speak our language. To this world we exist only on paper.

I feel like the six-year-old boy I was fourteen years ago, sitting in a seat like this one and fastening my seat belt. I look around me and I see familiar surroundings. I see my mother's face next to me smiling. Although her face has grown tired and old, the smile is the same as it was fourteen years ago, full of hope and reassurance. It is amazing how all these years have passed and I feel exactly the same: confused, puzzled and, yes, still wondering what life holds for me.

Rebecca

Amira Soliman
Yasmine Sobhi
Sarah Naguib
Malak El Shazly

I was born into the Shilouk tribe in Malakan, a city on the Nile in the south of Sudan. Malakan is a poor city where most people live in huts and only the very small wealthy sector can afford to build homes of concrete or stone. My family, like most, was very poor. I never knew my father; he was a sailor and he died of a sudden illness before I was born. The first four years of my life we lived in Malakan, though I remember very little, if anything at all, about the place. Then we exchanged our hut for a two-room house with a courtyard in Khartoum. My older brother gave up his education and took charge of the household, which consisted of my mother and I, and my younger brother and sister. It is a custom in my tribe for a widow to have sexual relations with her husband's brother or best friend, which explains how I later acquired a much younger brother and sister. But at this point in time, there was only my mother and three younger children, and my oldest brother believed, correctly, that he'd be able to provide a better life for us in Khartoum.

Khartoum was bigger and brighter than Malakan. What I remember most are the bright colors in the streets, the shops, the signs, and in the clothing. The people themselves seemed happier, as if they were experiencing something that those in Malakan had lacked. The variety of clothing, the reds and greens and yellows, may have had something to do with this sense of joy I felt while watching them move about in the streets. In Khartoum, Muslim women wore headscarves but Christians were not obliged to do the same unless they were in school. Though bright colors were sparingly permitted and women in Khartoum could not wear short skirts or pants. I remember when I was a child, I almost cried with joy when I was allowed to wear a bright red dress to camp. Later, when I was older, I was arrested for wearing a short skirt that was, in truth, not very short. I was not physically harassed. The police were very respectable but they told me I would be whipped thirty-five times if I was ever caught wearing unsuitable clothing again. Needless to say, I was not arrested by the 'wardrobe police' again.

My mother never learned to read or write and she never worked. She was emotionally distraught from the loss of my father early on, and later from the problems with my brother, which meant she could not take on the duties of head of the family, and which may have caused her death in 1993. Perhaps because I took care of my younger sister and brother in her absence, I developed my interest in humanitarianism. I always wanted to help those who were less fortunate. Even as a young child, my dream was first to become a human rights lawyer because I saw so many injustices done, especially to Christians. As a Christian myself, I experienced some of this persecution, which was more severe in the Muslim north.

Even as a very small child my life revolved around church. My mother had taught me prayer was a way to become close to God. That proximity made me feel safe, so I prayed more and more. As my involvement with the church deepened, I decided I wanted to become a nun. Later, I would change my mind in favor of a husband and family, but as a young girl, I thought that becoming a nun was the most important goal I could achieve. The more difficult life became at home, the more I turned to church. In fact, religious fervor in Sudan was to a great extent measured by the pain that people suffered as a result of the war. Before the war, we were not that religious, but we learned to use religious values as a means for survival, to understand how to cope with what was going on around us, and to cope with the challenges we faced.

And life did become increasingly hard for all of us. My older brother, who found a very good job in a foreign company that imported machines, began to drink. He married, but instead of becoming more stable and responsible, he drank more and beat his wife, and me and my sister too. My mother suffered from seeing her son in this state and the constant state of agitation that his actions brought upon her made her physically sick. During my brother's violent outbursts, I would run to the church for comfort. The priest told me to pray for my brother and to be patient. At least the church was safe and quiet; it was my sanctuary when I could no longer bear to be at home.

My childhood in Khartoum had a few pleasures. I loved sweets, anything with sugar, though these were rare, as we had no extra money. And I loved my toy dog, Ahsoul, who was named after a friend of mine who had died. This was a tradition in our tribe, to name someone (or something) after a recently deceased loved one. What I loved most of all was helping to ease the pain of others; perhaps it helped to ease my own pain. I went with my church to hospitals to visit sick children and to prisons, where we brought food and medicine to both Muslims and Christians. To me, the essence of Christianity is to give support to all people, regardless of their religion or race. But after we would leave the prisons, after visiting Muslims, government officials would run to ask them what we had said, thinking that we meant to convert them, which of course we did not. The government knew that our church owned cars that were used to take us on our prison visits, as well as to other outreach programs, and one day they took these cars away from us. At one point, the priest at my church asked me to stop helping Muslims, to give first to other Christians, but if I found a Muslim in need, I could not do anything else but help him. I wanted to help all people, as Jesus did, according to the Bible.

Not everyone understood my desire to help Muslims, since Christians in Khartoum felt the impact of religious discrimination. My family could not afford to send me and my sister to a private Christian school so we attended a public government school, which forced all students, Muslim and Christian, to veil. During religion classes, Christian students were permitted to leave but we did have some lessons in which we memorized verses from the Qur'an. On the other hand, I felt safe in Khartoum. I received little, if any, physical or verbal harassment on the street and I wore a cross around my neck every day. In the north, I heard about Christians who sang and danced on the streets on Christmas Day and the police made them stop and go inside; they said Christians caused chaos. As a result, we had to file for permission with the government in order to celebrate our holidays publicly. My family celebrated Christmas quietly with friends and family, eating *manghakino*, a plain flour and water pie eaten with fish that is a specialty of our tribe. I did not like it though, I preferred sweets, which we seldom got to taste.

My social life as a young girl was restricted not only because of lack of funds but because my brother would not allow me to leave the house. I could not go to cafés or movies with friends, even if I did have the pocket money to afford it. My brother told me he made these rules for my own protection but as I got older, I realized his capacity for violence as his drinking became worse and worse. I began to hate him and I always blamed him for the excessive emotional stress that caused my mother's death. I did not graduate from high school until I was twenty-two, which is not uncommon among southern Sudanese who study in the north. Many children like me often do not begin school until age eight, or even nine or ten, so it takes more time to complete the courses. In large families it is not uncommon for girls to drop out of school at age ten to help care for the younger children in the family. I enjoyed school and being with my friends, and my favorite subjects were religious music and theater. I loved to sing and I wanted so much as a child to become a nun. But when I failed my final exams and went to work in the church, teaching catechism classes to children who were studying for their first communion or confirmation satisfied my need to help others, and I realized that I might continue to work in a church and get married and not become a nun after all. I went back to school, while continuing to work, and two years later I took my exams again and passed them.

I was arrested the year I graduated from high school. The government security forces would go from house to house looking for alcohol and if they found it, they would arrest every person in that house, even the children. My brother, of course, had his share of arrests. One day, I was visiting a neighbor when one of these raids took place and when alcohol was found, I went to jail too. I was insulted, although not physically abused, and released the same day. But it was a frightening experience.

For the next nine years, I lived my life in much the same way I'd grown up; focusing on church activities and praying that my brother would stop drinking. In 2001, I was in the northern city of Ren, at a church service with an Italian priest and another Sudanese layperson. I was speaking the word of God when two men in civilian clothing, not military suits, came into the church and arrested us. The charges were unclear but during the interrogation I realized that the police thought I was a spy from the Sudan People's Liberation Movement, the southern rebels. I was taken back to Khartoum and locked up in a jail cell. The Italian priest was returned to Italy and the Sudanese layperson disappeared; I never again heard of his whereabouts. I was put in solitary confinement in a small room flooded with water. The only food I was given was too spicy to eat. It was my first time in jail and

I was terrified. They could do anything to me—they could torture or kill me. I prayed a lot. After four days, I was released. I went immediately to my church and found support from the priests and nuns there. They helped arrange for me to travel to Egypt on a ship to Aswan and from there by train to Cairo. The thought of leaving my family and my home made me feel paralyzed with fear. But what if I stayed? Now that I had a criminal record, what fate might await me if I was arrested again? I had no choice but to leave.

I cried all the way to Cairo on the train. I knew nothing about the city and I knew no one there. All I had was a letter from my priest, which I brought to Father Claudio at the Sacred Heart church in Abbasiya. I was able to find the church, which is known as *al-Kinisa al-Sudani*, or the Sudanese Church, because so many Sudanese live in the area nearby, selling hair accessories and crafts on the street and walking to and from the compound. Father Claudio was kind and helped me find a job teaching kindergarten at St. Luanga's, the refugee school that Sacred Heart hosts. He also found an apartment for me that I shared with two other women.

When I finally got the nerve to go outside, I expected to be treated as just another person, the way Egyptians in Sudan treated me in Khartoum. So I was shocked to find that Egyptians, especially young male adolescents, had so much hostility toward their African neighbors. At first, I stayed inside my apartment because, once on the street, someone would throw stones at me from an upstairs window. People also threw water and taunted me, calling me "donkey," "chocolate," or "prostitute." Even long after I arrived in Cairo I was chased in the metro by teenagers who threw stones. But I have been in Cairo for seven years now and I must say that the violence and harassment against African refugees has decreased, perhaps because Egyptians are used to us or because our numbers lessened as some of us resettled or returned to Sudan.

One year after my arrival, my younger brother and sister joined me in Cairo. Once I had my family members with me in my own home and I had a job, my life began to stabilize. I realized that there was less discrimination against Christians in Cairo. In Sudan, Christians are discriminated against in the workforce but in Egypt there are Christians in very high positions. Of course, in the informal economy it is different. For example, Muslim maids receive better treatment from their Muslim employers than Christians do. And the standard of life in Egypt is much higher than it is in Sudan. But so are prices; my apartment in Maadi costs LE 700 a month but I only make

LE 600 a month, so I am forced to always ask for loans from my church. And while I love having my brother and sister here in Egypt with me, my younger brother has a way of getting into trouble. He had an accident in a car that he had borrowed from an Egyptian friend, and was taken to the police station and asked to pay a fine of LE 200. Of course, I had to pay it as he is uneducated and makes very little money—and LE 200 is a big expense for me.

Two of the most momentous events of my life came in 2005. First, I met my husband, Sam, on Christmas Day, when he came to my home with some of my relatives. He soon proposed marriage but I refused because I knew so little about him. I knew he had been a doorman who was studying to become an Anglican priest. After one year, however, I got to know Sam and accepted his proposal. Our wedding was held in the Anglican Church in Ataba and all my friends and relatives came to the traditional service, complete with Sudanese music and a Sudanese priest. Your wedding is supposed to be the happiest time of your life, but I was terrified of the responsibility of marriage and the family I would create. But, at the same time, I was happy. Sam and I even saved up enough money to go to Alexandria for a honeymoon. Three months later I became pregnant, but it was an ectopic pregnancy and I was fortunate to have surgery that saved my life. My doctors tell me I can get pregnant again and I pray that this will happen.

The other momentous event of 2005 came when African refugees occupied Mustafa Mahmoud Park. I did not camp in the park but I visited people who did. They settled there for three months, men, women, and children from many different tribes—both Christians and Muslims—to make a statement to the UNHCR; they wanted resettlement. They did not want to remain in Cairo and they could not go home to Sudan because, for many, there was no home to go back to. I want to make it clear that I never did support this occupation of the park. Their problem was with the UNHCR, not Egypt. It is not Egypt's responsibility to give them money, or visas to go to Canada. But by taking over the park they took advantage of their host country because what they did was not legal. It also did not help their cause.

I remember the day that the police arrived and forced the refugees out of the park. I had cousins who were camping out there with their six-year-old. When the military buses pulled up and unleashed hundreds of policemen who led a baton charge to force out the refugees with water hoses, my cousins and others inside the park at first thought that these buses were to take them to the airport to go to Canada. They called me and told me this and I was so excited that I packed my few possessions and hurried to meet them, thinking I would go to Canada too. But by the time I arrived in Mohandiseen, the police had formed a barricade around the park and no one was allowed in.

The police were asking everyone to vacate but there was no response. They then asked for the women, children, and the elderly to leave. Some of the pregnant women and mothers with small children did want to leave at that point, but the refugee leaders refused to let them out. The police spent three hours begging the refugees to bring the children and the elderly to safety and warned that there could be danger if they remained. But they were stubborn and insisted on staying. What struck me about the people in the park was the strong sense of unity this diverse mixture of religions and tribes had created; it was a unity forced by the discrimination that all refugees experience, and by the impending disaster that this discrimination, if left unchecked, could bring about. But disaster did come, and it was not the fault of the Egyptian police.

I blame the refugee leaders for not allowing or encouraging their people to leave when the police warned them about the attack. They were told what would happen, and they refused to give in, at the cost of so many innocent lives. I did not see it happen. I did not want to. When I could not get through the police line, when I realized that these buses were not taking refugees to the airport but to somewhere much worse, I went home. You could smell the danger in the air. I was free to go to safety and many in the park were not, and that was the biggest crime of all. I went home and watched the violence on television. I had been there when the tension was mounting and knew that the only possible outcome was blood and horror. The shrill cry of babies separated from their mothers, the howls of mothers whose babies were torn from their arms, even though I had known that the situation would be horrific, I felt shock go through my body. Even before I got the next call, telling me that my cousin's six-year-old son was killed, crushed between police leading the baton charge and his own family, or beneath the masses of either group, I felt a sickening dread. It was the culmination of the terror that had been rising in my stomach ever since I went to the park earlier that day. If it was wrong for the Egyptian police to storm the park, causing the deaths of innocent children, then what was the right thing to do?

The future of the African refugees in Cairo was not solved by the Mustafa Mahmoud Park incident. They did not get a magic ticket to America, Australia, or Canada. Some refugees heard reports of good jobs, healthcare, and schools and so they went to Israel. I would never consider this option, because there is no peace agreement between Israel and Sudan, which means I could never go home again. Sudan is my home, make no mistake about that. My sister, though, left for Israel in April 2008 with her fiancé, who has a friend who works for the Egyptian military and who helped them cross the Israeli border. They were arrested, taken to a camp, and detained. When they were released they went to the UHNCR, where they got an interview and learned about job opportunities. So perhaps they will stay. But they are the lucky ones; other refugees save their money and pay Egyptian traffickers to smuggle them across the border. They place their trust in these people who take their money and leave them on the roadside to die or to be deported. This should give you an idea of how miserable life in Cairo can be for refugees, that a refugee's dream of a future could lead him to take such risks.

And what are my dreams? My great hope for the future is that I can go home to Sudan, to Malakan, where I would like to open a nursery for the children who have no parents to care for them. So many children go unattended and then grow up and begin roaming the streets and causing violence. But there are nurseries in Sudan funded by private organizations and churches. Once I save enough money, I'd like to fund one of these organizations and start my own day care center. My husband supports this idea, which came to me when I saw the nurseries in Egypt and how much good they can achieve in terms of child development, and he wants me to succeed. Of course it will take time, but I am patient. And I have a talent for hairdressing, which can help to earn extra money. Don't let me forget my most important dream: I want to have children. I want to send them to school and encourage them to study at universities. I will tell them my story and about the obstacles I faced and overcame in Sudan, and then in Egypt, and all the troubles I learned to overcome in order to learn from my experiences. And what I learned, I will teach them, because it is important for them, for everyone, to know that the world is a dangerous place when you are vulnerable, when you are displaced. But I have hope. I have always had faith. I believe that the world can be made better, but only by the people who live in it.

Ibrahim

Nora Eltahawy
Hebbah Hussein
Mustafa Ebeid
Marlene Shaker

My story starts in Khartoum, where I grew up with my family: two brothers, a sister, and our mother and father. Back in the day, before the Sudanese traveled to the Gulf for money and learned to love buildings, we all lived in houses. The heat would be overbearing at times and people would grow irritable, but what I remember when I look back is a loving, close-knit community. Growing up, I was as free in the houses of my aunts and uncles as I was in my own. There was no such thing as calling ahead of time for scheduling visits. We shared our houses the way we shared our lives, and when I would get sick of my house, I would sleep over at my relatives'. Even though we weren't related, I remember how kind our neighbors were to us as well. I remember the time my family traveled to Syria for a few weeks. I was knee-deep in university exams and so I stayed behind, and every single night my family was gone, our neighbor would come over and invite me to eat dinner with her family. Sometimes, because she knew how busy I was, she'd wrap some food up and bring it over instead. It's memories like these that make it so hard to understand how some people in Cairo don't know their own neighbors.

I grew up in a democratic household, in which everyone expressed himself and in which our parents would convince us of the 'rules' rationally. One time, when our father wanted to change the color of our car, he went around the house asking everyone's opinion. It was only after he'd discussed every little detail with us that he made any changes to our car.

Another incident I remember is of me slacking off. Back when we were kids, I was the one responsible for dropping off and picking up my sister from school every day. One day, a group of my friends tried to convince me

47

to stay back with them and leave my sister to go home alone. "I wish I could, but what am I supposed to do?" I'd replied, "I have this burden of a sister I have to deal with."

As soon as we got home, my sister told our father everything she'd heard me say to my friends about her. Typical of the way he treated us, my father didn't hit or yell at me. Instead, he sat me down and explained why he always asked me to pick up my sister and how it would be dangerous for her to go alone. His talking to me that night convinced me more than any punishment could have, and I never complained about my duties toward my sister again.

I lived out my childhood at a time of civil unrest and war. I suppose I always knew there was something wrong with my country, even when I was very young. My family was as political as it was democratic, and I grew up listening to my parents talk about everything that was going wrong in our nation. My father was always incredibly active in politics and the first taste I had of the type of life he led came by accident. On the way to the store one day, sent to buy some matches for my mother, I saw a huge crowd form at the end of the street. There were probably a thousand people there that evening, all waving their hands, or holding banners, or shouting slogans. I knew it had something to do with the government, against which those people were protesting for freedom and for their rights, so I wandered into the crowd for a closer look. I was so enthralled by what was happening around me, I didn't notice the time and it was a few hours before I finally got home. My mother, naturally, was out of her mind with worry and it was a while before I could get her to focus on my question: "How can those people be wrong, Ummi? How can they all be wrong and one man be right?" My mother laughed. She never answered my question.

As my friends and I grew older, the reality of our lives changed dramatically. Instead of spending our summer days swimming in the Nile (which we called the sea back then), more and more of us were being drafted for war. Military service, for many of us, became inevitable. Although I was never drafted myself, I remember the day our neighbor's son, a close friend of mine, got the news that he was to serve in the military before he would be allowed to enroll in university. On his way to the military camp, my friend's bus overturned, breaking his ribs and landing him in the hospital. I remember visiting him there, and how it broke my heart to watch him struggle to take a breath. I left him that day to run a few errands, and when I came back he had passed away.

Our neighbor's son wasn't the only person I lost to the war. When we were seventeen, another friend of mine got drafted and was sent to join the army. I don't know if my friend ever fought in battle, but what I do know is that his standard-issue boots were too small for his feet. And I know that when he complained about them hurting him, his sergeant hit him on the head so many times he died shortly after. His death—the death of a brilliant young man over something so trivial—was incredibly hard for me to accept. I knew I loved Sudan but at that point, I watched Sudan being poisoned.

Not surprisingly, it was around that time that my social and political activism became more serious, and it was also around that time that I first got arrested. As sophomores in high school, a group of friends and I, who were known to be opposed to the government's programs, were put in charge of organizing the school's cultural week. In the middle of organizing the events, a representative from the General Union of High School Students (a notoriously pro-government society) requested the addition of a paragraph to our program that would state our support of the country's regime. We rejected the amendment, which consisted of jihad songs and pro-government propaganda and our program was published in its original form.

At the end of classes that day, around four in the evening, my classmate and I were stopped near the school gate by what appeared to be four policemen in civilian clothing. Threatening violence if we resisted, the officers drove us in their box car to the headquarters of the General Union of Sudanese Students. Inside, a group of older students, who I believe belonged to the Islamic Front, immediately became violent with us. Interrogating us on our stance and questioning our denial of their amendment to the school's program, the men accused us of violating government policy. After four hours of beatings and accusations we were finally released.

The situation only worsened when I joined university. By that time, my father had already been arrested and imprisoned. But even his eventual death in custody didn't curb my political involvement. As a freshman in university, I simultaneously declared a major in computer science and joined the Democratic Union Party and the Democratic Union's Student Association. As my involvement in the organizations grew, I became responsible for editing press statements and political literature and eventually was chosen to monitor the student elections on campus. During one year's elections, the National Democratic Alliance (NDA) defeated the Islamic Front and chaos ensued on campus. Claiming the election results were false, the Islamic Front and its supporters began clashing with any opponent they saw. When the security forces intervened, it was the NDA supporters—myself included—who were beaten. I lost consciousness that day and was hospitalized.

The fight continued for a long time. By the second day, university officials intervened and shut down the student union until, they said, the election results could be "verified." A month into the suspension, I joined a group of students in rallying for the return of the student union. Typical of their role in all rallies, security forces appeared on the scene, brandishing sticks and iron bars. A friend's arm was broken, and we were all beaten and sent to the security office. It had become a sort of routine: our isolation in the security offices and our abuse at the hands of the officers. Their methods of torture this time were clubs (the bottom of my feet were beaten so badly I could barely stand upright) and paper; we were only released that night after signing an undertaking to stop our activities.

Signed undertaking notwithstanding, when I was asked to speak at a political rally shortly afterward, I accepted immediately. In my speech, I attacked the government's ostracizing of dissident voices and called for the protection of the individual freedom and human rights laws enshrined in international conventions. What I called for that day—what we were all calling for everyday, really—may have been simple enough in theory, but it was also what led to my downfall in Sudan.

The day after my speech, my name was found on a list posted on the main gate of our university. The people on that list were all accused of blasphemy and secularism and the notice concluded by legalizing the shedding of our blood. The Democratic Union Party acted almost immediately. Hiding me with the student secretariat, the organization did its best to protect me and the rest of its members. But the police knew where to find me and, this time, when I was driven to their offices, I was alone.

In their office and over the course of several long days, I was insulted, beaten with rubber hoses, kicked in the head, made to stand upright whenever I began to fall asleep, deprived of going to the bathroom, and given only a scant portion of food and water—it was the middle of the summer—each day. I was interrogated every day. The accusations were many: seeking to convert from Islam, cooperating with international opposition, seeking to overthrow the government. I was accused of treason and told I would be court marshaled and sent to stand trial under the national security law—under which the sentences are either life in prison or death.

They continued in their attempts to torture answers out of me, and I continued to refuse to speak. When it became clear that I would stand my ground regardless of the pain, the officials finally took note of my failing health and I was sent to a nearby military hospital, accompanied by a personal guard. By this time, the Democratic Union Party had taken steps in arranging my departure from Sudan and their plans were furthered by a relative of mine who happened to work in the military hospital. A day before my planned escape, my mother visited me in the hospital where she smuggled in some civilian clothing for me. The next day, my relative-doctor took it upon himself to distract my personal guard and I was finally able to slip away.

The union had arranged with a Sudanese Airways officer to facilitate my departure from the country and, sure enough, the officer made sure to sneak me onto a departing flight through the staff entrance. I arrived in Cairo on August 19, 2003.

Race has always been a big thing in Sudan. Back home my skin color—dark, yes, but light enough to be considered Arab—meant I was luckier than many. It's true that the Christian south has been abused at the hands of the Muslim north; I, myself, have heard stories of southerners being taken as slaves to the northerners. But what people don't realize is that I, like many others, grew up listening to darker-skinned Muslim northerners being taunted. Those with darker skin are referred to as 'abd, a colloquial term for slaves. The mistreatment of the darker-skinned Muslims drives home the message that in Sudan, the darker you are, the worse you will fare.

Knowing all that I know about race dynamics from my home country, maybe I shouldn't have been surprised by the way we are treated in Egypt. Things work differently here, but I learned fairly quickly that pretending to be from Aswan would get me more respect than announcing my true nationality ever could. I also saw that, once again, my skin color would save me from the plight of darker-skinned refugees. I ride the Cairo metro often and I remember one incident where a southern Sudanese man stepped into the same carriage I was in. I immediately could sense the change in the Egyptians around me. It couldn't have helped that the man's choice of fashion—braided hair, pierced ears—were so different from the Egyptian norm, but judging by the Egyptians' sneers and the sarcastic cries that followed him as he walked through the carriage ("Watch out for Burkina Faso!" and, "Here comes Burkina Faso!"), this was more about skin color than his choice of accessories.

The men on the metro may have left me alone that day but my skin color counted for nothing in my dealings with the UNHCR. I use the past tense because at this point, three and a half years into my stay in Egypt, I have given up on the organization's services. For a while, contacting the UNHCR became a ritual of my life and my frustration at getting nowhere led me, like so many of my fellow refugees, to join the organized sit-in. Everyone may know about the raid that ended our sit-in; still, it's hard for me to convey the horrors I saw around me that day and in the days that followed. Families were spread out among prisons and it was hard for parents to find their children. NGOs had begun sending workers to help us out in the prisons. By the time we were allowed to go to the morgues to see if they held anyone we recognized, I was able to go with an American aid worker, Courtney, from a local NGO. At the morgue we met a refugee who was there to identify his son. Courtney and I, in an effort to support the grieving father, asked if we could go in the morgue with him but the policemen refused. Even after she asked me to explain to them that all she wanted was to do her job, to stand with the man when the body was brought out, we weren't allowed in. So I stood outside, Courtney crying at my side. It was the hardest moment of my life in Cairo.

In the aftermath of the attack, and after most of us had been released from prison, I remember a traumatized widow asking me for money to catch a train back to Sudan. The woman's husband had been killed the day the of the attack and, like many others who were abused at the hands of the Egyptian police, they'd weighed their options and realized they preferred to return to persecution in their own country, that woman only wanted to go home. I tried explaining to her that the UNHCR was supposed to give money to families of deceased refugees but she interrupted me: "Will it bring my husband back? It would be shameful for me to accept that money. My family and I are better off without it."

With everything that had happened to us at the hands of the Egyptian police, I knew that going back to the UNHCR offices, where police cars lined the road in front of the gate, had become more intimidating than ever for us refugees. I tried to do something about it and, for days, would spend hours on the phone, only to be transferred to a voluntary repatriation section where the staff didn't care about what I had to say. I kept trying and, eventually, when I was connected to an Egyptian officer in the UNHCR office, I tried to control my frustration long enough to explain the importance of why I was calling. "Men like the police officers in front of your gate have been killing people from our community," I'd explained, "how are you supposed to regain our trust?" But the man only lost his temper: "Do you know what would happen if Egyptian refugees ever went to Sudan and organized a sit-in?!" he'd asked. "They would eat us. They would eat our very flesh."

That was probably the moment I decided to give up on the UNHCR, and so, when another worker contacted me a few days later and wanted to go over my file, I went in with no desire to discuss my case but with the sole intention of asking her to relay a message to her boss. I explained my frustration of writing to the UNHCR six or seven times, only to get no response. I explained the situation so many of my fellow refugees, destitute and homeless, found themselves in. And more than anything, I explained my feelings regarding the atrocities that happened at the sit-in, explained how the UNHCR, in my eyes, were as accountable as the Egyptian police about the lives lost in the breakup of the demonstration.

"You could've intervened. You could've sent anyone from your staff to speak to the police and they would've left us alone. You could've saved lives. But those people are gone and your organization hasn't even issued an apology about the lives lost. You should be ashamed. All of you should be ashamed."

I left the woman crying that day. But she promised to tell her boss.

It's been two years since our sit-in was attacked and I've seen many refugees come and go. Relocation isn't for everyone—I don't think it would fare very well with me. So I stay in Egypt and I do the best I can. At times I work as a translator for different embassies; other times, I work with NGOs around the country. Eventually, I'd like to read up on all the advances in computer technology that I've missed because of all this.

I may have gone through a lot of changes these past few years but when people ask me what I yearn for, my answer is always the same: Sudan.

Melissa

Jaida Abul Fotouh

I am a southerner, but I have never lived in the south. My parents came to Khartoum from Juba, in southern Sudan, to escape the horrors of the civil war in the early 1960s. My father had a difficult life. His parents were killed in the war and he was uneducated. But despite his lack of formal knowledge, he had a strong work ethic and he understood the value of an education and made it a personal goal to send his own children to school. This is one of the reasons he worked so hard. He had a good job working for the military in Juba, but the rebels in the south had no regard for the government, and they assumed that my father, who, like them, was a southerner and a Christian, was a traitor. In fact, my father did not support the political views of the north; he was simply trying to make a living for his family. He knew that he was not safe in Juba, so he moved to Khartoum, returning later only to marry a southern woman from his own tribe—the Bari. My parents went to the north, where I, the first of four children, was born in 1962, in Omdurman.

Omdurman was a poor Arab neighborhood, and the neighbors that surrounded our tiny house were all Muslim. From my earliest days I remember the persecution we experienced as Christians, as if we were not only different but also inferior. What I remember most is the discomfort and pressure I felt as a result of being 'the other' when I was a child. Even before we were old enough to go to school, my younger sisters, my brother, and I were pressured by our neighbors to convert to Islam.

My father had a job but he was not well paid and we were poor; my parents struggled to keep us clothed and fed. Our one room house had a courtyard where we cooked over an open fire and ate together on the ground. My parents slept in a tent, and we children rolled out mats in the house. The outdoor bathroom was not even an outhouse; it was a hole in the ground. While we had a simple life, it was not an easy one. I should remember the sounds of the city around me during my childhood but it's as if I was deaf to anything but the fear pounding in my own heart. I grew up in Khartoum, away from the war in the south, but I did not escape the psychological impact of the war because it had scarred my parents and they could not hide their scars from me. It is as if the war was just outside my window and I could hear the screams of a mother watching her children die or the blast of sudden gunfire. My parents told me stories so dramatic, so graphic, and so frightening that I remained in a constant state of fear. This fear was compounded by the discrimination that we, as Christian southerners, experienced from our Arab neighbors.

The only time I felt at ease was on Sundays, when we went to the local Catholic church and I could play with other children who were like me. There, I knew peace. When I remember my childhood, I remember looking out the window and making wishes. I don't remember what I saw outside the window, but I remember what I wished for; I wished to be happy.

One of the things I wanted most in the world was to go to school. I saw other children my age with their book bags every morning, on their way to class, and I desperately wanted to be one of them. My parents could not afford to pay for a uniform or books, let alone the tuition, but because my father was determined to educate his family, my mother began selling *fuul* sandwiches (which are called *tassali* in Sudanese) in the street, and with this scant extra income, my education began. I began my studies at age six, which pleased me very much, but made my father very angry because in the primary level we were taught only one thing: to memorize the Qur'an. Children who learned quickly were rewarded, as an incentive, with sweets made of dates. I loved candy, which we could never afford at home, so in no time at all I had the Qur'an committed to memory. My father, a devout Christian, was furious and managed to get me enrolled in a Christian school, which cost more money and was farther from home.

I loved my new school; every day was like Sunday because I felt comfortable and safe knowing that no one would punish me or taunt me for having a different faith. I excelled in my studies, especially Arabic, because my family spoke our tribal Bari language and I felt inferior until I could speak and understand the language of my country. I was a diligent student and did well in my other classes: math, geography, history, science, and especially art. My academic performance was enhanced, probably because I felt a sense of belonging and a connection with my new friends. We played games and climbed trees and because we had no money for toys, we drew pictures of animals and landscapes and trees, which we would sometimes give to a special friend as a gift. I developed an interest in art and loved to draw. Art supplies were scarce but there was no shortage of subjects. I drew flowers, as well as the chickens, dogs, and goats that lived in our courtyard.

One of my happiest childhood memories was getting up early in the morning to milk the goats. Goat milk was a staple of our diet, along with cornmeal and beans. When we were low on money and could not afford meat, we heated sugar and water and added cornmeal, stirring it until it became a kind of pudding. There were times when even basic food like bread was too expensive. We accepted this, though, and learned to do without.

I had plenty of reasons to be miserable as a child. We were poor, we suffered discrimination, and even after I transferred to a Christian school our neighbors pressured my sisters, my brother, and me to convert to Islam. We also felt the impact of the war, albeit our experience was secondhand. But there were also times when I was deeply happy. I believe that my father is responsible for bringing this happiness to us because he taught us how faith can bring hope and even in the worst of times we found comfort as a family. When I turned fifteen I needed all the comfort I could get because my life took a sharp turn. With two younger sisters and a brother, my family could no longer afford to pay for my school tuition and uniforms. I felt ashamed when I had to go to school in ill-fitting regular clothes and this affected my school performance. I was not entirely angry when my parents told me I had to leave school, but I was shocked when I heard the reason why: I was to marry a thirty-year-old man—an accountant who attended our church—a man I had no feelings for one way or another. A stranger.

Our wedding took place before we'd even had a chance to exchange words. But I was not angry with my parents for arranging my marriage. I understood that this was my obligation; I'd been a financial burden to my parents for many years and this was something I could do to help relieve some of the pressure. Besides, I discovered that my husband, when we finally met, was handsome and kind. He, like me, was from southern Sudan, he had a university education, and worked in an accounting firm as a consultant, so he made more money than my father. But I was too young to understand what marriage was. I just didn't get it. I moved into a house very much like my parents', not too far from them so we could visit often. When I looked out the window of my new house and made a wish, it was to have a family of my own, and that wish was soon answered. I had my first daughter at age seventeen, and four more quickly followed.

For a few years the future looked bright. My husband had a good income and I supplemented it by crocheting tablecloths, towels, and linens and selling them to shops. I also got a job in a nursery and was able to take my children with me. I was determined that my children would have a good education. And they did. My husband received a promotion and went from his accounting firm consultancy to the Ministry of Finance, to the United Nations in Juba. It was still too dangerous in the south to bring the entire family, so he'd go for three months then return for a visit. This went on for years, and we were happy. Until one morning, when my husband was away, I got a call from his office. They told me he had been arrested and was in the political prison in Juba. What a shock! At this time, I had five children and I was pregnant with the sixth. It occurred to me that he might not be released from prison and that I might never see him again. But I did. He was released and returned to Khartoum, but he was a changed man, unstable and uncomfortable. Even though he'd been released, security officers followed him everywhere and he refused to sleep at home, thinking they would come for him in the night. He told me he wanted to leave the country, which scared me. Where could we go? How could we afford the papers and the tickets for our large family? We knew no one outside of Sudan.

And then he was gone. My husband disappeared. I was seven months pregnant, alone and confused. I could only pray that he was all right. At night, the government security officers would come to our house, knocking loudly, and turning the house upside down in their search. They made such a mess and they frightened my children. It was horrible. I didn't know what to do.

Finally, I got a call from my husband. He'd fled to Cairo and he'd made arrangements for his brother to get papers for a tourist visa so that the children and I, and my husband's five-year-old brother could join him there. Then, like so many refugees, we'd let our visas expire and remain in refuge. We would not return to Sudan. But I barely had time to register the fact that I might never see my parents or my homeland again because I was too busy selling every stick of furniture, every pot and pan—literally everything we owned—to raise money for our plane tickets to Cairo. Even after I had sold everything in our house, we didn't have enough money for all the plane tickets, but some Christian neighbors gave us the rest. I told them that I needed the money to give to my mother, because I didn't want anyone to know our plans.

In order to leave Sudan with no one knowing we waited until late at night to go to the airport. My first wave of fear came when the airline officials refused to let me on the plane because women in their last term of pregnancy aren't allowed to fly. I told them that I was only in my fifth month—I was really seven, almost eight months pregnant—and they reluctantly let me on board. But even then I worried; what if they were right? What if air travel could damage the unborn child? And what would happen when we arrived in this strange country that I knew nothing about? What if my husband was not there to meet us? I had nothing in my pockets. Even if my younger children cried with hunger, they would get nothing to eat, because I did not even have money to buy them biscuits at the airport.

When our plane finally landed in Cairo, we got through customs with our tourist visas and collected what little luggage we had. I scanned the lines of people waiting to greet new arrivals. My heart pounded with dread. But there he was. My husband stood waving and my children ran to him. I was in a new country, I could not go home, and I had no money and would soon have a sixth child. There were plenty of worries ahead but I forgot them for a moment. I felt only relief at the sight of my husband.

However, this moment did not last long. The feeling of security and hope disappeared as soon as I remembered that I was in a foreign country where I knew no one except my husband, and where I trusted no one except my family. This feeling of confusion was augmented when I realized that my family and I were going to stay with a friend of my husband and his family. The apartment in Dar al-Malak in Abbasiya was small and narrow—with only two rooms for fifteen people—but we had no choice. We arrived in May and remained there until July 23.

My husband found work as a housekeeper in the mornings; however, his salary was not enough to support us all and consequently he took another job in the evening, teaching English in Sakkakini (Sacred Heart) Church.

Unfortunately, the stress and anxiety I was experiencing made my pregnancy more complicated and, hence, I had to have a cesarean section, despite the fact that we could not afford it. Fortunately, our kindhearted priest was able to collect money so that I could have the surgery. I delivered an adorable baby boy.

Now that our family was even larger, we had to move. The apartment we shared with our friends was extremely small to accommodate such a number of people, and our children and their children were not on good terms. We moved into a one-room apartment, where we felt more comfortable and had more privacy. We needed money so badly that I found a job for my oldest daughter to work as a housekeeper. We paid for our rent and basic utilities with the money my husband and daughter earned. Meanwhile, I made sure that my children applied to St. Luanga's, the Sacred Heart church school.

Finally, my family was leading a normal life but I still felt confused, insecure, and unable to face the reality that I was living in a foreign country, where I would probably spend the rest of my life, and where I would raise my children and start a new life. I still could not consider Egypt my home. Life was difficult and harsh due to discrimination, and we felt no sense of belonging, or security. My children were full of anger and fear. They felt discrimination from Egyptian children on the street. For them, Egypt was a strange country, which did not welcome them and they desperately wanted to return home. At first, they did not make friends. They never felt happy and their eyes always showed disappointment. But slowly they began to feel more confident, as they went to the church playground and met other refugees. They went twice a week from five to nine in the evening, which distracted them and cheered them up. School was the most comfortable place for them because they felt normal among the other Sudanese children and that gave them a sense of equality. I felt happier because my children felt happier.

When I arrived in Egypt in May 2005, I found out that my husband had applied to the UNHCR for Refugee Status and got a yellow card and an interview on July 25. However, due to the peace treaty in Sudan, our interview was cancelled. In 2006, we were accepted as refugees by an NGO which provided us with LE 500 every two months. We suddenly stopped receiving this aid when the NGO lost its funding. We needed more money, so I found a job in a nursery and started to sell handcrafted towels that I made in my free time. As a consequence, we were able to move into a larger apartment consisting of two rooms, which gave our large family more space.

For me, Egypt is a sanctuary. I love the fact that I can walk freely in the streets without having any fear of being killed by a bomb or a radical group. When I look around, I see safety and hope. However, despite the peace of mind that this sanctuary brings, there are obstacles that I cannot overcome, which make me feel stuck with no choices and nowhere to go.

My children are not attending an accredited school. St. Luanga's curriculum and the certificate it offers are not recognized in Egypt. Therefore, while they learn to read and write and can gather some knowledge, which can help them understand life and perhaps have a better future, they cannot sit for exams and go to college. Despite the fact that my children read and write beautifully, how will they ever be able to apply for an appropriate job? What future do they have? Although they are young, they understand the limitations of living in Egypt as well as I do. I have noticed that as they get older, my children become more depressed. They understand that they are refugees who had to flee their home country due to war, and they grasp clearly the reality that they have nothing here: no identity, no careers, no educational opportunities, not even basic respect from people on the streets, let alone in the government. No wonder my children are confused. They also live in fear and anxiety due to the potential violence of gangs that are found not just on the streets but also in schools. These gangs sometimes attack the school with their light one-hand weapons and begin to cause chaos and terror. The problem is that no one can react or do anything. This problem hit home when I realized that my husband's brother had joined a gang, which terrified me but confused me even more. I did not understand how he, a child who had escaped violence and come to safety, could begin to renew that cycle of violence. I raised him the same way I raised my own children but he dropped out of school and joined the gang. His decision not only disappointed and depressed me but in fact terrified me. My heart pounded and I could not sleep well. I feared that my oldest son, who was the same age as my husband's brother, would come under his influence and join a gang too. I tried to talk to my husband's brother, telling him that his gang status was not acceptable, despite the fact that I was afraid of him. One night, his rival gang broke into our home to fight with him. That was the last straw. I told him he could no longer share our home.

My daughter dropped out of school to work; her employers were cruel and harsh. She told them that she wanted to quit her job, and the Egyptian wife—who was angry because she did not want to lose a good, hard worker—accused her of stealing. In her next job, a housewife made her work longer hours without giving her enough money. She had offers to be a live-in maid, but I refused. I know of Sudanese women who are raped or killed when they accept such an arrangement, because they become entirely vulnerable to the family that hires them. However, because she has no other choice, my daughter still works as a housekeeper. We need her salary and because she did not finish school, she won't be able to find other jobs.

Our current dilemma is whether we should stay in Egypt or return to Sudan. Although the peace treaty was signed, peace is not yet a reality in my home country— though I wish it were. There is still war in Darfur and between various tribes. The tension and fierce competition between politicians for important positions in the system is fierce, and extreme poverty and desperation lead to corruption. This tension and ongoing conflict terrifies and confuses me because I want to go home but home is not yet a safe place. So I remain in Cairo, in limbo, where nothing terrible can happen to us if we are careful, but it is guaranteed that nothing good can happen either. My children cannot go to college and become doctors or lawyers. We are the dark-skinned 'other.' And so we wait. We cannot risk all that we have achieved to return home and yet I must go home. I worry about my ageing mother because I was not able to reach her when I called and I don't know what to do.

The Egyptians treat us cruelly because of the color of our skin. They call us "Chocolata" or "Buya Bong." Once they made me so angry that I returned the insult, which led to a serious fight. However, the Egyptian police took us all to the station. Now when we are insulted or affronted we usually do not react because we are not able to defend ourselves legally and, even if we tried, it would have no consequence. We are black-skinned. We have no power or money. We are guilty. Our landlord knows that we are refugees and raises the price too high, aware that we can't afford to pay it and also aware that we cannot afford to complain or fight it. When the rent is not paid on time, we are all dragged out of the apartment. There is no sympathy at all for us. Hence, we try our best to save the money for the rent and we don't eat much so we can take the money saved for the food and use it to pay our rent.

My husband's illness is another problem that is hanging on our shoulders. Last year he became gravely ill and we did not know what to do or where to go. Our church provided treatment because the hospitals were expensive, and thanks to Caritas, a Catholic charity that paid for his medicine, he is stabilized but is not completely well. But his health problem is another reason why I don't want to return to Sudan because there we possess nothing and there are few jobs. How could we make ends meet? How could I afford to give my husband medicine in Sudan?

Despite all these problems, I try my best to lead a normal life. Everyday I wake up at 6am. I pray for twenty minutes and I read the Bible. I go take my shower and get dressed. Then I go and wake up my children so that they get dressed and go to school. We have breakfast, which is usually only tea with milk and, if we can afford it, some bread. I go to work from 8am to 2:30 in the afternoon, return home, and wash and cook for my family. My children nap in the early evening and if I go out, I let them sleep. Sometimes I go out to sell embroidered towels which I make in my rare free time and other times I go out to meet with other wives. At 9pm I go to the market—if I have enough money—for milk, sugar, and bread. When I get back home, my youngest are already asleep and my older children will tell me about their day and we go over their homework. At night, I make sure that my husband has taken all his medicine and then take a shower. If there is food, I eat. And finally, I pray and try to sleep.

I love my children and they are my life. I can't live without them and I want them to get the best education possible, to have a better life, a better environment and a future better than my own. But my husband is sick, and I am afraid to remain in Egypt, where my children have no future because we are invisible, because we do not count. I want to migrate to Australia, Canada, or America. Anywhere will be better than Egypt. We tried to leave to Australia when we found out that the Australian embassy sponsors and supports refugee families but we were not successful. Still, we did not give up. Our daughter has a friend, who left to Canada and was able to get us a sponsorship offer. Unfortunately, we were rejected due to the claim that there is no reason, no problem that keeps us from returning back to Sudan. Officially, there is peace but in reality there are landmines waiting in the fields, there is tension between tribes, between government officials and people, there is corruption and no infrastructure, medicine, or good schools. You would think I would be used to rejection, to the sound of still another door closing behind me, as if my life was a long corridor of closed doors. More doors will open, and already I can hear the click as these doors shut too, and yet I keep my eyes open. I keep waiting for new doors to open.

George | *Riham Morsy*
Bishoy Demian
Mustapha Salama

My father was a rich man by southern Sudanese standards, rich enough to marry three women. In Africa polygamy is common, even among Christians like my father, for whom multiple wives signify affluence. A man who has three or more wives is clearly prosperous and in fact, my father supported a large family of fifteen daughters and eleven sons. He did not inherit his money, but earned it by focusing on his agricultural studies, followed by hard work. He dreamed of running his own, large farm, and after he completed his high school education at a local missionary school, he was accepted at the Institute for Agriculture in Yambia. His first job took him to Juba, where he worked first for the Department of Agriculture and then as manager of a coffee plantation.

It was there that he met and fell in love with my mother, who had a job picking beans in the fields. After they married, my father got a better offer that took them to Nimula—a city in the far south where the Nile enters Sudan—which is occupied by our family tribe, the Ma'adi. I was born in Nimula, but have few memories of it because we moved to Obo when I was three years old and my father received another, more lucrative job offer as a manager on a government farm there. Encouraged by his good prospects, my parents began to raise a family. But my father was very ambitious. He saved his money, which must have been difficult despite his good job because my mother's father had died young and my parents helped to raise her younger brothers and sisters and put them through school. Yet, somehow, he saved enough to buy his own coffee plantation in Obo, and it was this enterprise that made him wealthy.

No family could possibly have enjoyed life more than we did in Obo. Life is better there than in other parts of Africa because there are more rainy seasons, making the land more fertile and yielding, and the people are happy because they are fed. It is also extraordinarily beautiful, with rolling hills and valleys. From the higher points, one can see miles of lush greenery, rich with government-planted mango, guava, and pie-pie trees. Obo is also paradise for children because they can always play outside in the perfect weather.

My parents took a close interest in their growing family; they wanted me to get a good education, so they transferred me from my first overcrowded primary school in Semes to the Baltaka Mission School, which was more expensive but had smaller classes and better teachers. It was also five miles away and because walking was the only form of transportation, I woke up at 3am. when the rooster crowed, and walked to school in the dark. By the time I walked home, my feet would be so sore and swollen that I had to pour hot water on them. To save me this excruciating pain, my parents arranged for me to live closer to school in a Norwegian church where my aunt worked, and arranged for me to come home once a month to visit my family. I was very satisfied with this arrangement.

For the next four years I was very happy. I loved my studies and my friends at school. We played football, sang, danced, and ran in marathons. Then, while I was home on vacation during a school break, my family learned that a war was moving around Sudan, staged by rebels who burned villages, and killed their inhabitants. Not long after, we learned that the rebels were in the nearby city of Winch Kaboo. Local government soldiers were prepared to attack, and we braced ourselves for the coming war. It came suddenly; when the fighting began we could hear loud gunfire all afternoon. The wounded came limping back, their blood and sweat making a kind of garish sheen on their arms and faces, and the number of so many wounded soldiers struck fear in our hearts. The rebels advanced to Obo, breaking into shops and looting, while shop owners ran for their lives. To replenish their forces, the rebels would knock on doors, looking for young men to recruit, breaking in if no one answered, firing guns. Heavy fighting raged for weeks, while we all lived in terror. To escape the gunfire, we hid in the deepest part of the valley on our farm, and slept in the bush for safety because we were more afraid of the rebels than we were of the lions, snakes, and serpents that lived in the bush. At least the animals didn't hate us.

The rebels had a pattern; they would fight for weeks, then leave, but they always came back. When they left, we'd go home but our hearts were always heavy with fear and the knowledge that they would return. When they did, we retreated to the bush. I remember trying to sleep outdoors, listening to the sound of gunfire, watching the bright lights from tracers, the phosphorescent bullets that the soldiers used for visibility, as they pierced the night sky. When morning came, we heard the engines, and knew the government troops were moving. Every night, two or three civilians died, because the rebels fired into the bushes. My mother had taught me to protect myself in heavy fighting; she told us not to run, but to scramble away by hugging the ground.

Life during wartime was harsh; we had no basic commodities like soap or sugar or salt. When someone heard there was salt available, they would go and buy twenty kilograms, or as much as they could carry, and sell small portions for high prices. Whenever the rebels returned, they would take away whatever salt or soap they could find. But we were resourceful; we squeezed the liquid out of the pie-pie plant and used it for soap, and we dissolved the remains of burnt hay in water and left it to evaporate; whatever remained we used as salt.

The rebels' pattern of leaving and returning was devastating because they always came back in increasingly larger numbers, attacking civilians and the government soldiers in our town. The fighting became more aggressive and several members of my family died. One day we were in our house, and someone—to this day, I don't know if it was the rebels or the government, because the two armies were not distinguished by their uniforms—locked us inside and set the house on fire. My mother, brothers, and I cried for help, and when the roof started to fall down, we were certain that we would die. It was my mother who saved us; she pushed down a wall, weakened by fire, with my baby brother tucked under one arm. The wall finally fell. We prepared to run for safety, but stopped short: a line of armed rebels stood behind the smoking remains of the wall, pointing their guns at us. My mother caught a bullet in one arm, and fell to the ground. One of the rebels raised his gun to shoot her, and I felt my heart freeze in terror. I'd seen rebels grab small children and throw them into the fire while their mother cried and then the soldiers would shoot the mother. Even though I had little hope she would be spared, my brothers and I cried and pleaded, and the soldier let my mother go. She did not waste a minute. "Run!" she shouted, "Save yourselves!" We scattered in different directions, without a chance to think that we might never see each other again.

Our entire village was burning, and there was nowhere to run but the forest, which became my temporary home. I lived alone there for a week, perhaps longer (it was difficult to distinguish one day from another). I was lonely and afraid, and I was starving. I picked fruit from the trees but there was no drinking water except for a murky stream full of frogs and worms. I was so thirsty I didn't care how dirty the water was. I pushed the worms out of the way and scooped up the water in my hands. At night, I had no matches but I found dried wood and soft grass and built a fire by rubbing sticks together, to keep warm. I needed protein to survive and at the time I did not know that worms were a source of protein—and even if I had, I don't know if I could have made myself eat worms. I did, however, eat poisonous snakes. I had to be very careful when I caught them, stabbing them with homemade spears, aware that if they bit me, I could die. They were also hard to catch because these deadly snakes only came out at night, but because they spread a glowing substance on the ground that attracted insects, they helped me track my dinner. And dangerous as they were, the snakes kept me alive.

I owe my survival in the forest to my mother's training. When we knew the war was coming, she told us that we must get used to living under harsh circumstances or we would die. She made us work on the farm and gave us difficult tasks that were physically exhausting. On certain days, she gave us no food for twenty-four hours. Some of my lazy brothers, who did not believe her and ignored her instructions, suffered. She had a true vision that became a sad reality, but because I listened and believed, I became strong. I survived.

I knew I could not remain in the forest, where I might be attacked by the lions and elephants that lived there. I waited until my village was completely destroyed and nothing was left but ashes and corpses, because only then was it safe to leave. I didn't know which way I was going, but I found myself in Torit, an unfamiliar city where I knew no one. I had no idea where anyone in my family was, only that my father was in Juba. But how would I find him?

Torit was considered a safe city at the time, but the road was lined with soldiers who immediately arrested me. They wanted to know why I was traveling alone and what had happened in my village. I told them the truth. They accused me of lying and of being a spy—even though I was only ten years old. Finally, they began to ask local people if they knew who I was. Fortunately for me, a good friend of my father's lived in Torit and he was among the locals that the soldiers questioned. He told them that he knew my father, assured the soldiers that I was not a spy, and promised that he would take care of me. And he did.

I spent two weeks at the home of my father's friend before we set out to find my father in Juba. Juba was also a safe city, though the journey from Torit was considered dangerous. Soldiers lined both sides of the road, and rebels had planted grenades at water pumps and wells. Because we knew this, we did not stop for water even though thirst was a persisting pain. By the time I arrived in Juba, my eyes were so swollen from dehydration that I could barely see, and my legs were still full of cuts and bruises from my week in the forest. But I forgot how much my body ached when I was reunited with my father and three of my brothers.

Two months went by before I was fully recovered. Then, for two years, my life was normal again. It was 1990, and I lived with my father and uncle and studied English and other basics in order to get back into school. I passed a placement exam and started special classes at the Sadaka School for children displaced by war. The school was so crowded it held two sessions: morning classes were taught in Arabic for the locals and afternoon classes were taught in English for displaced children, most of whom had learned English in their native villages. But it was very difficult to absorb information in class because one classroom held as many as 130 students. My father realized that I was not getting a good education and once again made the decision to put me in a smaller, more expensive school, and I did very well there. But despite my good grades and stable home, I had a gnawing worry; I still knew nothing of the fate of my mother, my sisters, or my other brothers. But this fear was soon eclipsed. By 1992, the war had come to Juba. School closed, and once more, I had to concentrate on only one thing; staying alive.

It was late at night when the war broke out in Juba. Bullets flew and a store selling ammunition caught fire and exploded in a burst of bright light. We didn't know where to run to avoid the heavy artillery, but luckily, we decided not to stay inside, because our house was demolished in the night by the tanks that moved through the city. I remember them rumbling slowly, chains red with blood, entire human limbs and pieces of flesh caught in the links. The next morning, my uncle, who had stayed with me throughout the night, sought in vain for surviving family members, while I went out to look for food. This was dangerous, because I could have been mistaken for a rebel and shot, or I could have been shot by a rebel. In the morning light, the streets were a horrible sight to behold; dogs and ducks were feeding on the dead bodies. I found no food. Instead, I was attacked by a police officer who kicked and hit me with his gun, threatened to kill me, and accused me of being a rebel. His soldiers put me in chains and I was sent to an underground detention area where my cell was so small I could not move. I managed to sleep until I was awakened and accused again of being a rebel. This time, I was given a choice: I could go to Khartoum, join the army, and fight the rebels, or I could be killed. I chose Khartoum.

I was blindfolded, taken to an airport, and put on a plane. I expected to arrive in Khartoum, but I knew immediately, though the blindfold was not removed, that I was in the north, near the country. Instead of being taken to an army camp, I arrived at a remote farm to care for goats. I was desperately hungry. I had not eaten for days, but I was told that I would share meals with the goats. Once more, my life changed. The Muslim farm owner told me I was now a Muslim and demanded that I observe the pillars of Islam. But nothing could change the feelings in my heart, or my own faith in a Christian God. I was told that I was a slave, and that I must obey or die. I thought that if I went through the rituals of an obedient Muslim, praying and fasting during Ramadan, that I might gain some respect, but my employer—who did not really employ me so much as he enslaved me—continued to beat me and insult me, regardless of how hard I worked. I slept with the goats on a bed of straw and ate the slop that the goats were fed. I was treated like a goat and I began to feel that I was a goat too. My life was miserable and I missed my family more than ever.

I spent a year on the goat farm with no idea where I really was. I knew that escape was the only solution but I was unsure how to find my way to safety in this unfamiliar region, where I had no sense of local geography. But I did make a friend, and he helped save me. I would take the goats to graze in the fields, where other goat herders—also southern Sudanese enslaved by northerners—tended their flocks. One of these goatherds was a very old man, who, like me, had been forced to convert to Islam. We were not allowed to talk to one another and it took a long time to realize I could trust him. Our friendship grew slowly. But once we began to talk, he became my friend. He told me about a major highway that led to Khartoum that I could walk to in about two days. But he made it very clear that if I was caught on the journey, I would be killed immediately. But I had been on the goat farm for at least a year. What did I have to lose? At this point, my health was poor and I had little strength. I knew that if I remained where I was, I would certainly die. I had a choice: certain death, or freedom with a risk of death, which is not a choice at all. Anyone in such a position will choose freedom and take the risk. Once the decision was made, I worked quickly to prepare for my departure. I hid some bread and a bottle of water, and on the appointed day, no one seemed suspicious. That night, when everyone was sleeping, I said goodbye to the goats and ran to the main road until I was out of breath. I rested for a few minutes and kept going. I did this for two hours and when morning came I hid in the bushes where no one could see me and slept a little. I waited until night fell again and continued running. In four days, I saw the main road. But no one had told me which direction to take to get to Khartoum.

Many cars went by before one would stop so I could ask for directions; the old man was right, this highway was a busy one, with trucks and cars moving at high speed. Finally, a truck driver stopped; he wanted to know who I was and where I was going, and why I didn't have any money. I told him I'd been robbed. I decided that this would be my story. He took me as far as he could, then I got another ride, then another. When I saw a checkpoint in the distance, I got out and walked away to avoid interrogation. I kept walking until I found a small village where people stared at me because I was a stranger and because I must have looked ragged and fearful. Children cried and ran from me. I passed this village and came to another, and then another, before I found the courage to ask where I could find a church. All the villagers were Muslim and no one could help me. Finally, a man led me to a Catholic church, where a kind priest listened to my story and gave me food, water, and a place to sleep. I remained at the church for one month helping with church activities until a group of priests on their way to Khartoum offered to take me with them. I was able to finish my journey in safety.

In Khartoum, I was taken to another Catholic church where I lived and studied in the church school. I was in my early twenties by the time I finally had my high school certificate. I could have remained in Khartoum and found a job or tried to go to college, but I wanted to return to Juba and find my family. The priests who had taken me in bought me a plane ticket, which made my journey easier. Once in Juba, it was not hard to find my uncle's family. My aunt and cousins were happy to see me, alive and well, and when they told me that my uncle had been transferred to Torit, I suggested that we all go there and find him. They liked this idea. We made the journey safely. I began to think my life was changing for the better. My uncle was delighted to see us; he now owned a successful sorghum farm, which also produced okra, tomatoes, and fruit. His main problem was that he didn't have enough workers, and so our arrival was fortuitous because we were able to help him. For two years life was stable and even good. Finally, I thought, the hard times were behind me. Then it became clear that my uncle was very sick. He was diagnosed with heart disease and the Sudan Council of Churches (SCC) made arrangements to take him out of Sudan to Syria for medical attention. I was asked to go to Syria too, to help my aunt take care of him. We all traveled to Khartoum, where our travel documents were being made, but while this paperwork was being completed for our departure, my uncle died. We canceled our travel plans and returned to Juba to bury him.

As the oldest male family member, it was my responsibility to care for his wife and three children, so we returned to the farm in Torit and remained there for one year. Then, the inevitable war broke out around the city. Overnight, rebels and government soldiers began shooting at each other and Torit was caught in the crossfire. Houses in Torit were set ablaze, and civilians were told by the army commander to evacuate to Laconda in the south. But on the road to Laconda we were faced with heavy artillery, which killed most of us immediately. The government was on one side of the road and the rebels were on the other; once again, we were caught in the middle. Yet somehow my family survived. Corpses littered the road and the night air was heavy with the smell of blood and the sound of women screaming. The piercing cries of children were the most painful. Yet I felt that it was these sounds, horrible as they were, that kept me alive, protecting me as I moved forward, as if they were tangible, insular, and somehow shielded me from the gunfire killing people around me.

Those of us who survived could not afford to walk. We ran. We ran to the Gouton Mountains to hide in government barracks, stayed one night there, and set out for Juba the next day. It took three days to get to Gumba, on the outskirts of the city. There was a great deal of chaos and confusion there. The roads were crowded with vehicles belonging to NGO's, that had come to rescue and feed displaced people, and military trucks and civilian cars. Two men asked me to help them bring food to the people coming from Torit. I agreed and left my aunt and her children to join the men in the back of a pickup truck. But before we arrived at the Juba Bridge one of the men told me to lie flat in the back of the truck. I asked why and the other man took a small gun from his pocket and hit me on the head. "You don't know us," he said. I was then kicked, beaten, and blindfolded before they removed me from the car and took me to an interrogation station.

I was left alone for hours. That night they came back to interrogate me and accused me of being an agent of the SPLA rebels. My head was bleeding badly at this point and they offered me no medical care. I learned they were government officials, who thought I was a rebel. I was held for what seemed like hours, and it was midnight before I got to the interrogation room and was accused of preaching against the government. They tortured me so much I didn't know who I was. I was kicked and beaten until I was unconscious. I was taken to a foul-smelling cell with a blood-smeared floor. There were two buckets in the cell: one was a toilet and one had water to wash my face. I remained in their detention camp for two weeks, eating nothing but scraps of food that were often so rotten they were putrid, until I was finally taken to Khartoum. There, once more, I was interrogated and tortured when I refused to admit to being a rebel spy. Finally, I was released on the condition that I become a spy for the government—I was to go and find the rebels and report on their activities. Once again, I was blindfolded and taken to a new location in the city; when the blindfold was removed, I discovered I'd been taken to the Sabah orphanage.

Any hopes I had of finally getting a meal at the orphanage were quickly dashed. The orphanage was really only a shelter and only offered orphans a bed, not meals. During the day the children were released to beg for food on the streets. I asked the watchman if I could go out and beg for food too, but at first he refused. If I did not eat, I told him, I would die and would not be a useful spy. Finally he agreed and I was allowed out. I was given scraps and leftovers at restaurants and once I had eaten, I asked for directions and found a Catholic church. The priests there were sympathetic when they heard my story and agreed to help me get back to Juba to find my family. They kept their word and took me in until they could buy me a plane ticket. But at the airport my ticket was confiscated by a corrupt official, who made me chase him from one office to another. Finally, I was arrested in the course of this chase and taken to the same interrogation camp where I'd been tortured before. Once again, I was tortured, kicked, and beaten so hard that I passed out—until I woke up in severe pain, to find boiling water being poured on my head. To this day, I have bald patches as a result of the scars.

After one week in this detention camp, I was returned to the Sabah orphanage and asked to report on those who had 'helped' me. Once again, I managed to escape and this time I did not need to ask directions; I remembered where the church was and found it quickly. The priests were alarmed when I told them that I'd been captured again. This time they promised to make sure that I got out of Sudan safely by buying me a train ticket to Egypt. First, they sent for my passport from my aunt's house in Juba to Khartoum. I remained with them until it arrived and boarded a train to Aswan. I felt a mixture of relief and anxiety because, while I finally knew that I would be safe, I did not know how to live from day to day without feeling the fear that had become a part of me.

The route to Aswan from Sudan begins with a train to Halfa, then passengers change to a boat and cross the border. Only when I had crossed the border and was truly out of Sudan did I feel a bit more secure. I landed in Aswan late at night and was the last person to get off the boat. I was alone when I went through customs—and perhaps this made the custom officials feel they could get away with it, or because they knew I was a refugee, they knew I had no recourse regardless of who witnessed the crime—and they robbed me, taking what little money and possessions I had. That was my introduction to Egypt, to the way the Egyptian police and many people treat refugees from Africa. The confidence and hope that I had been trying to build up quickly dissolved. I started to panic, fearing that the Sudanese security officials could find me and return me to Sudan. Fortunately, I had put a little money, just enough to take a microbus from Aswan to Cairo, in a pocket that the customs officials did not manage to steal. But this was a small comfort. During the twelve-hour journey to Cairo, I felt alone and afraid.

The microbus dropped me off in Abbasiya, a working class Cairo neighborhood, where I was happy to see many Sudanese people on the streets.

I asked one of them where I could find a church and he directed me to Sacred Heart, which locals call Sakkakini. I walked into the compound, which serves as a refugee center and also holds St. Luanga's, the largest refugee school in Cairo, which enrolls over one thousand children. I was taken to meet the head priest, Father Claudio. He was scheduled to travel that day but despite his busy schedule he took time to hear me tell my story. He must have heard so many refugees tell stories like mine, about the horrors they endured in Sudan, but as he listened I watched him and I could tell that his compassion was genuine. I gave him a letter from the priest in Khartoum who had helped me, verifying my story, but I could tell that Father Claudio believed me. Father Claudio gave me LE 60 and told me how the Sacred Heart refugee center could assist me with work training programs, medical care, and legal issues. Already, I felt less lonely and afraid. And then, in the church courtyard, I was reunited with my childhood friend Peter, from Obo. He introduced me to a family who agreed to let me stay with them. This was the beginning of my new life.

Now, I live in an apartment in Arba Wa Nus, a slum area near Nasr City where the poorest of the poor, Egyptians and Sudanese, live together. The streets are not paved and some apartments have dirt floors and no plumbing or electricity. One apartment building may hold as many as fifty people who share one bathroom. For the first two months, Peter's family helped me pay the rent. Meanwhile, I began to mobilize other Sudanese to start the United Sudanese Student and Refugee Association (USSRA). Our objective was to build a school and an AIDS awareness program. Finally, I was working, though I was not being paid. I was told that when donations came in, I could pay my rent, so I managed to evade the landlord's requests for a few months until our USSRA school opened. I began teaching children, a work that I love. A group of Japanese journalists came to visit our school and wrote an article about it, which was published in Japan. As a result, we received US$400 in donations, which was enough to pay my back rent and the rent for the school building. In this way, I have continued my life, and dedicated my time to helping my people. The children of Sudan are the future of our country and what could be more important than their education?

My life is stable now, good sometimes. I learned from a friend that my mother is alive in a Uganda refugee camp with my youngest brother and one sister. I still don't know if my father is alive or dead. Some of my siblings are abroad and some are missing. My family has been torn apart. Despite the horror it inflicted on so many families, I believe the war in Sudan is both good and bad. The bad is obvious: our ancestors were given knowledge and power by God, and the current leaders have misused this power. Rather than worshiping God, they made people worship them. So God took away their intelligence and they began to fight and kill one another. But this war made people realize that God exists and that this war is His punishment for not honoring and worshiping Him. Many innocent people lost their lives, children became orphans, families were broken up, and people, like me, were torn away from their homes and from the people they loved. And yet there are some happy endings to this war story. I know, because I am alive to tell it. I am telling my story because I want the world to hear my voice and the pain that it carries, and because I want the Sudanese to realize that the solution to our problems is not guns, but God. It is only through God that we can find peace in this world.

Nkosana

Ahmed Abou Zeid

Watching the sun go down over Lake Tanganika; sitting in the shade of eucalyptus, acacia, coffee, and oil palm trees; the sweet fragrance of the clean air; laughter and music at large gatherings of native Burundians, who play football and volleyball in a central court.... These are the only images that I can remember, or want to remember, from my childhood, before the civil war started in Burundi.

Here in Cairo, my life is so different. Sitting in a café in the working-class neighborhood of Abbasiya with an Egyptian student my own age, I notice that people look at us strangely. Are they staring because they have never seen an Egyptian sitting down for coffee with an African, or of the two walking together down the street? Perhaps they stare because they cannot imagine what an African and an Egyptian have to say to each other. "What do these people have in common?" they might ask. But to answer this question, they would have to know who Africans really are.

What Egyptians know about Africans is only what they see on the streets and in the media. On the streets of Cairo, they see lean dark men and women walking alone, eyes down, trying not to attract attention, and perhaps succeeding so well that they become invisible. They see young black-skinned men in groups, wearing baggy hip-hop clothes, moving to the beat of music, an earpiece tucked into one ear. Egyptians also define Africans based on what they see on TV, in the American rap videos shown on Arab channels, in which Africans are depicted as wild, primal creatures, pulsing to the beat of hip-hop music, making erotic dance moves with beautiful, almost-naked girls. And then they are mythologized into heroes. What male teenager anywhere in the world would not dream of being a black rapper, infused with the strength and power of pure rhythm? I am nineteen and I am African but I am not a rapper. I wear a blue shirt and jeans. I am from Burundi, a country I cannot bear to remember.

I remember this: I loved my mother a lot, and I know she loved me more than anything. But she, like every beautiful thing in my life, disappeared as a result of the civil war that began when I was seven-years-old. The war left me with an everlasting wound, under my eyes, when an enemy soldier hit me with the back of his weapon and injured my face. Some wounds heal, others do not.

Life was very simple for me as a child, perhaps because we were poor. My father was a driver and my mother did not work outside our home. I had an older sister who was married but she died of an illness when I was five years old. Her husband left Burundi for Egypt so we did not keep in touch with him. I don't remember visits to the homes of any friends or neighbors; for me, my mother was the world. I have almost no memory of my life before the civil war, but I have a vague sense of the place where I spent my first seven years. I know that it was somewhere in Bujumbara, Burundi's capital, and that I spent my childhood in a neighborhood there called Chibitoke. Our house was very simple, made only of wood, and like most houses in the country, it consisted of just one floor. In Egypt, people live in large, concrete structures, but in Burundi, entire neighborhoods are composed of small, independent one-story houses, a layout which creates more space, more sky, and more room for children to play. And we made good use of it: kicking a football in the street and swimming in a lake about two hundred meters from my home. Playing football and swimming—that was an ordinary day for a child in Burundi.

I remember the day the war came. I had left my mother that day, and went out to play with some friends near the lake. In the middle of our game we were shaken by a strong, unfamiliar voice. We looked, but saw nothing, no one. Who was this powerful speaker? His voice told us nothing, only that he was not one of us. We continued playing but with some anxiety. That voice, so bold and commanding and strange, frightened us and sent a quiver of tension into the air. A few minutes later, we looked again and this time we saw where the voice came from and we saw hell on earth. Strong men wearing jeans and shirts, not uniforms, carried guns and machetes. There were many, a long line of senseless killers, breaking down doors, destroying houses. People scattered in random directions, creating chaos. And the invaders, who I later learned were called Asaye, killed everyone, both Hutu and Tutsi, and not just the men, but even small children and women. They killed, and then they stole the property of the dead. I saw scores of people die in just a few seconds, more than I could count. And what did I do? How did I react? What happens to people who see such things? These are questions I could not answer for years.

What I witnessed in that first violent outbreak of genocide in Chibitoke made me much older than I'd been earlier in the day, but part of me still felt very much like a small child. Yet, in the midst of that horror, I became responsible for what I'd seen. I inherited a kind of power I never wanted nor understood.

In Burundi, there are two main tribes, the Tutsi and the Hutu. The two tribes began to fight one another, arguably, because there was undeniable injustice in the distribution of resources between them. You could compare the Hutu to communists, who wanted to create an even and just distribution of goods between the people, and the Tutsi to the capitalists. They lived in luxury and kept the Hutu in a state of oppression. We all know what happens when a people is oppressed: they will, if they can find a way, fight their oppressors, and the Hutu did just that. They began a war against the Tutsi. But the problem between the tribes must go much deeper because over time the fortune that the war was fought for was distributed in a fair manner between the two tribes of the country, and yet the river of blood is still running.

It is important to describe as many circumstances of my childhood that I can recall in order to understand the impact that they had on my ability to feel, to experience a normal range of emotions, such as I did before the war. I am talking about love, depression, nostalgia, desire. I know what these words mean, but I cannot experience their meaning. My ability to internalize emotion is gone. It stopped on the day that the war began and I was left with only one feeling: the will to survive. I have no ability to feel but I have a very clear understanding that nothing in life is guaranteed, that there is no such thing as an unconditional promise. It is impossible to feel peace, to have a sense of security, because such sensations, the tranquility of peace and the reassurance of security, were gone in one shotgun of a second: that strange, strong voice that I heard by the lake killed my ability to feel. I escaped, but

I was not completely intact. The blood of the murdered children, their cries, the screams of their mothers, and the act of witnessing these casualties of war became a part of me. It made me a casualty of war too.

The memory of a child is very strange, especially when that child remembers seeing dozens of people brutally murdered for reasons that he cannot understand. In my new state, isolated from feeling, my memory holds only small, contained recollections, like capsules, compressed so they cannot haunt me. Plain facts uncolored by emotion that could drive me mad with grief and sorrow. Because, simply to recall what I have seen, to replay certain images in my mind, would give them the power to recreate a horror I cannot bear to contain.

If you went to Burundi as a tourist, you would never be able to distinguish between the people who form the two tribes. How are they different? Maybe the Tutsi like to listen more than to speak, while the Hutu talk all the time. My mother is Tutsi and my father is Hutu. They fell in love and got married before the civil war started, exactly like an American love story in the movies, in which true love is threatened by the horror of war. But the war ended that love story just as it ended my ability to understand my present or my future.

I remember that we were invaded by the enemy but I don't know who that enemy was. Had my mother's tribe come to kill us? Or was it my father's tribe, representing the rival, and would they kill us too? And where did I stand between these invaders? I honestly don't understand the real reason for this war but I understand human nature and man's ongoing search for fortune and power. In all wars, the tribal, religious, and racial, differences are never the entirety of what makes a war; it is the hunger for material gain that persists time and time again. This is what happened in Burundi.

When I first saw the invaders wreaking havoc on so many innocent people, I wanted to run home to my mother, either to rescue her or so that she could rescue me. But it was too dangerous to reach my house; men on the street told me I would be killed if I tried to reach my house. To this day I don't remember if these men were policemen or civilians but they understood the danger and made a great effort to protect the children. They led us, on foot, to the Congo. If we tried to stop and sleep, the men in charge of us would wake us up. We arrived in a refugee camp for children only, but the situation there was not good; there was insufficient food and water, people would kick and beat each other to get the limited rations. I had to fight to survive hunger and death. I don't remember a lot about my life before or after the day I left Chibitoke but I believe we spent three or four months in the Congo. The camp held many innocents, including me, all of us struggling for survival. What do I recall about this time? I can remember the context, the situation, but the emotional heart eludes me because by then I had cut myself off from sensation. I had to do this in order to survive. Yet when I think back on this time, what I think about is this: what made us struggle so hard? What actual reason did we cling to, to justify our eager desire to stay alive?

One day we were told it was safe to return to Burundi. We went home the same way we arrived: on foot, and it was a gruesome journey. Dead bodies lay alongside the road, many without heads. Blood was everywhere. It was terrifying to see that so many people were dead all around us. I was taken to my home but my neighborhood was a place I barely recognized. Some houses were destroyed and all were empty. Only ghosts inhabited my street. My mother was gone and I feared she had been killed. Somehow I was able to bear this because I had gained a curious kind of wisdom. Now, although I still don't understand what it is that I know and I cannot give a valid explanation for why I attained this knowledge, I know something about war.

The man who was helping me took me to the small room where he lived in Bujumbara. Soon after, one of his friends came to visit and heard that I'd lost my mother. He learned her name and told me that he had seen her recently, which made my heart leap with joy. I was taken to her in Bwiza, a neighborhood in Bujumbara, where my mother was living in a small house with many other people. We both cried when we were reunited. We hugged each other hard. I couldn't believe how fortunate I was because I had been sure I would never see her again. There was not enough room for both of us, so my mother asked the man who'd brought me to her to help us. He took us to his house in Bwienzi, another neighborhood in Burundi, and we stayed there for three or four years. The city was still dangerous and schools were closed. My mother tried, but could not find a job and our host was unable to bring us food every day. I spent my days begging on the streets, giving whatever small amount of money I made to my mother. We remained in this situation until I was twelve or thirteen years old. I could not read or write.

My mother and I had to move because our host told us he could no longer support us. We went to Motakura, a more distant neighborhood in Bujumbara, and we found a very small palm-thatched hut in the woods, which was the cheapest kind of housing to be found. I continued to beg for money and food every day. My mother gave me some lessons and I learned to read and write in Burundi, but when she found a job as a housekeeper, these lessons stopped. I managed to attend school for one year, but I did not learn much; the school was crowded and there were no books. I might have continued but my mother's employer stopped paying her, which made it impossible for her to pay my school fees. Eventually I returned to begging on the streets. This area of Bujumbara was not dangerous but life was hard. I had to be careful to go to different parts of the city to beg because if I returned to the same spot, some irritable shopkeeper might hit me. In general, people were not kind to me. Sometimes they beat me and took what little money I had earned. But what could I do? I survived. My mother would ask me, when she saw my bruises, "Who beat you?" And when I would tell her, she would cry. She would brush away her tears because she didn't want me to see how much pain my bruises caused her.

Without any preparation, at age sixteen, my life changed completely. Finally, I saw a light of hope. We found my brother-in-law, who is older than me and who came looking for me to bring me back to Cairo, where he had a home. He succeeded with a great deal of effort to arrange for me to travel with him to Egypt. The legal process for Burundians to travel was expensive and complex and he was not a rich man but he persisted, despite the small chance of success. And he did succeed. If a filmmaker were to make the story of my life into a movie, this success would not convince the audience, the public, who would say it was too easy, it was a fairytale ending. But of course, it was not the end.

I had no knowledge of geography due to my lack of schooling, so when my brother-in-law appeared with his magical offer, I had no idea that a city named Cairo even existed or that there was a country called Egypt. The very word, Cairo, excited me; it promised me something beyond the mere escape from fear and sleep that had become my life. I hated to leave my mother but my brother-in-law could take only one of us and he chose me. I had to ask myself, would my mother be better off if I were to stay with her? Could I protect her from the invasion of the weapon carriers or from the risk of disease? But she wanted me to go. And so I went.

That space of time during which I was preparing to travel to Cairo was the first time since the outbreak of war that I didn't use sleep as a means of escaping fear. I felt that finally, there was a future for me. That future was still unknown but it held enough promise to make me keep my eyes open on the bus on the way to the airport. For the first time, I could allow myself to see the real world, everything that I'd blacked out into nothingness, into a blank slate. And this is what I saw: murdered bodies strewn along a sandy road. Not soldiers, but small children and older ladies, catastrophic scenes that I cannot remove from my mind to this day, no matter how hard I try to shrink them into a small package of color and sand. They are stubborn and they remain, life-sized, even bigger than life, and I cannot make them go away.

The bus passed the lake where I had been playing with my friends the day the war began; the lake where we used to swim, the lake that had water clear enough to drink. That clear water was now black and at first it seemed that the lake itself had disappeared and been replaced by a solid black mass. Then I realized that what I saw was in fact hundreds, maybe thousands, of Burundian bodies floating in the water. This is how I left my country. A glimpse of one of the ladies lying dead by the roadside recalled my mother's image to my mind and I felt a flicker of fear; was I leaving her to this fate? What future awaited me in Egypt? Would I find peace and understanding? As the bus sped faster toward the airport, past blood and sand, I felt a certain distance between myself and the other passengers, as they talked to one another or chewed gum or smoked. I felt that I was in a dream, in which I really had no control over my environment but was at the mercy of the dreamer's subconscious. Was I selfish to leave my mother? I had no answer. Even when I boarded the plane and looked down at Burundi for the last time, I saw it as an abstraction, a dark land, bright in parts with yellow light. I hate that color, yet I love my country, in the same way that I love my mother and wanted at that moment to go back to her. I still want to go back to her.

The dream ended and the space around me became my life again. And when the plane began to descend, I looked down into the golden lights of Cairo, more beautiful than the glare I had left behind in Burundi. How can I describe the impact of so much brightness, of the glitter that shone down on the earth below? The city expanded further and further, as if the lights were part of a randomly distributed package, lights of a new color, cheerful and inviting, urging me to dive deep into the river that their glow created. The plane landed and my relationship with this strange new city began. Everything was exciting, even the long, slow part, standing in line to get through customs, perhaps because I was so busy absorbing everything around me.

There were big-screen TVs, women in luxurious dresses, and the scent of fragrance. There were travelers from Asia, America, and Europe, though I could not have known where they came from, I knew only how different, how confident, and how exotic they appeared. But despite this mixture of people, this new wealth of light, I had an underlying feeling—now I could feel something again, just a stirring of emotion—of safety. I knew that I did not need to be afraid anymore. There was no reason to look quickly to the right or the left, to search for the enemy who might suddenly draw a gun out of his pocket, who might be pointing that gun at you, behind your back, at this very moment. It seemed, in this brightly lit airport, where people laughed as if they were at a party, that there were no enemies in Cairo. I walked out of the airport, the automatic door clicking behind me, into my new city, with my eyes wide open, because there was so much out there, and how else could I possibly see it?

If I thought that my life would change immediately for the better in Cairo, I was wrong. But I do not remember having any such anticipation. I had learned to erase any kind of expectation, even from my imagination. My introduction to Cairo was not a comfortable, easy transition because my brother-in-law wasn't able to host me in his house. He was not, as I said before, very well-off himself, which makes it so amazing to me that he spent so much time and money to take me out of Burundi, and to bring me to Cairo. He did arrange for me to share an apartment with other refugees from different African countries and promised to visit me and to send me money regularly. This was difficult for me, as I was used to living only with my mother, not foreigners. I felt the strangeness of being a foreigner in a new land and this was not modified by having caring people around to show me the new city, because my companions were new themselves, and not all of them were entirely trustworthy when it came to sharing money and paying the rent. None of us held work permits, and would have been hard pressed to find employment even if we had work permits, as Egypt's poor economy could not provide work for many Egyptians.

I lived in a city that I knew nothing about for months; I knew my way around my neighborhood but I really knew nothing about Cairo until I met a refugee lawyer at the UNHCR who helped me to enroll at the American University to study Arabic. This was a wonderful time for me and it was at this time that my real relationship with Cairo started. Because it is a complex city of intangible delights, if someone asked me today about what I like most about Cairo I would never find an answer. All I know is that the image of Cairo for me is as if someone coated it with the color of its golden lights, and when I think of this, I remember my first vision of the city at night, from the airplane.

However, I can easily find an answer for the thing I hate most about Cairo, which is the lack of human empathy. It is impossible for me to describe the feeling of insecurity that possesses me in the streets—if I fainted in a crowd, people would not come to help me. Why do people hate others? The world fits us all and it is possible for us to live together in peace. There are truths that make no sense, questions without answers. Why should I be a refugee and not a well-cared for son, beloved by parents who can support him and give him an education? Why should I know nothing about my parents' fate? Whether they are dead or alive? I have come to accept that constant change is part of life.

I was finally visited by my brother-in-law, who told me that he got a very good contract with a company in Qatar and that he had to leave Cairo within a week but he would continue sending me money regularly so that I could continue to live in Cairo. Even though I wasn't living with him, the news of his traveling increased my feeling of insecurity. My image of Cairo, the golden-lit city, was turning darker. Yet I survived until a few months later, when my brother-in-law was fired from his job and he sent me a letter announcing that he would not be able to send me money any more. The city and my state of mind went from dark to pitch black, as if nothing could ever become darker. Suddenly, I was truly alone, with no money, no job, and no residence. What do you have when you have nothing? You still have, I discovered, some small hope.

If you gave me a camera and told me to make a movie of my life, I would film my own story but I would try to make it lighter in content so that people would enjoy it while eating popcorn and drinking Coca-Cola. And I would be happy, even with an audience who was willing to spend two hours watching a drama that would be forgotten once they left the theater, and drove their luxurious cars out of the mall's huge parking lot, and continued their lives, which are so very different from my own. I would willingly show my wounds to the world, for the public to cry over, to exclaim, "how could anything be so horrible?" before they dry their tears and go out to expensive restaurants, to laugh and show off their lovely clothes. Because I still have that hope, so small it is arguably invisible, that one day my movie would have an audience, maybe only one person—but that does not matter—who would enter the cinema without holding his popcorn, and my film would urge him to think, not to cry. And this audience would think about a way to make this world better, and the film would stay with them and become a part of them, as my war, as my broken country, has become a part of me.

How can we save the world? This pain, this loneliness and agony, and my fear and the memories I try to shut down are a factor of world problems, not my own. We must fix this world. My problems could become yours. I am not so different from you. But how can one person change the world? These are questions that I want to ask, that I must ask of every audience member in every theater in the world, with everyone I meet, with every reader, and even of my own conscience. Can the world be a better place? Can people learn to be just and fair? Can all human beings ever enjoy freedom? Can love survive where there is hate? Can I dare to wish for a better life?

Can you enter the cinema without popcorn?

Mahzouz

Reem Amr

When I'm asked where I come from, my answer is always Sudan. This is true; I was born to Sudanese parents and this makes me Sudanese. However, I was born in 1984 on July 17 in Addis Ababa, the capital of Ethiopia. My parents left Sudan because my father was a soldier in the Sudanese People's Liberation Army (SPLA), the army of the Sudan People's Liberation Movement (SPLM). The SPLM went to war with the government in 1983 after the government in Khartoum failed to honor the Addis Ababa peace agreement of 1972 and imposed shari'a law on the entire country. This was generally regarded as a sign of disrespect targeted at Sudan's diverse ethnic and religious population. Because they were displeased with their government, my parents left Sudan for the safety of their two children, even before my birth. My parents left their home in Yirol, a village in south Sudan, which had become a war zone, in 1983 and moved to Ethiopia. In Ethiopia, I became both a refugee and an eternal optimist in a world that could be cruel and unfair, even to innocent children. This is the story of my life, a life that has spanned twenty-three years and has taken me through four cities in four countries that I called home.

My name is Mahzouz. That's what all the people I know call me. The name literally means 'fortunate.' My mother started calling me Mahzouz the day I was born because I was born in the bush. She struggled through labor alone with no medical assistance, and I got the nickname 'Mahzouz' because I was lucky to survive and I brought her a lot of joy. I don't remember the last time I used my passport name.

When my family moved to Ethiopia, I had an older brother and a sister. When I was six, my mother gave birth to a beautiful baby boy. Years later, he would grow up to look exactly like me. We are often mistaken for twins.

Because my father was a soldier, he had to leave for weeks at a time to go to the south and fight with the SPLA. He never shared his war experiences with his children. At the time, I was too young to absorb the enormity of the situation he was in. I knew he was fighting in the war but I didn't know that much about the war itself. I didn't understand what happens at war. I just listened to my mother and accepted his long absences. We were grateful he didn't come back in a coffin. Ever since I have been old enough to understand the civil war in Sudan, war has become a very painful and personal matter to me because my dad was a part of it. I used to ask my mother about my father's work, and she would only say that he went off to flight, that he'd be back soon. She was always convinced, or at least she convinced me, that he'd return to us again. And he always did.

Every time my father came back from the war, he would ask for me. He always wanted to see me first, to hug me and ask how I had been. We had a very special connection; I respected what he did in the SPLA. My mother always talked about him as a hero. I thought he was hero. He put his own life at stake for his country and his fellow countrymen. Being a soldier forced him to have a dual personality: one that would go to war and see the unthinkable and one that came home to us and played with me just like other fathers would play with their children. I remember we used to play volleyball and football a lot. I wasn't good at either of them, but my father was so good. He seemed to be good at everything he did. He was a good father, a great athlete, and an excellent warrior.

When I was born in 1984, refugees were protected by the Ethiopian government. At that time, there was friction between the Ethiopian and Sudanese governments and Sudan even launched several attacks on Sudanese refugees in refugee camps in Ethiopia. But nevertheless, Ethiopia hosted Sudanese refugees while Sudan hosted Ethiopian refugees, because this is the African way; as if the borders of each African country are so porous that despite our disagreements, we are all united in the name of Africa.

You might think that as a Sudanese refugee I would grow up feeling some degree of humiliation in Ethiopia but this was not the case—except on a few occasions. I did not feel like an alien. Even though I knew that Sudan was my own home country, Ethiopia was a comfortable place for the Sudanese to live. I spent my first ten years in a rented wooden house in Addis, in a peaceful neighborhood called Donna Danielle. The owners of the house had a son my age, named Azeke. Azeke was the kind of best friend we all want to have, and I spent many of my childhood days playing football and other games with him. I will never forget his loyalty; when all the other children at school mocked me because of my refugee status, he would defend me. We both felt that we were not only friends, but also brothers. For instance, I didn't like football but Azeke was very good at it and because of this, he wanted me to be as good as him. He never gave up on me, always encouraging me, even though I wasn't a very good player. I don't know why, but I never liked playing football or basketball even though you'd think I would, because I was a very tall child, and today I stand at seven feet. I come from the Dinka tribe, and we are among the tallest people in the world. Two Sudanese of Dinka origin play in the NBA, Manute Bol and Luol Deng. And people in the fashion world may be familiar with the tall, elegant Dinka model, Alek Wek.

I may not have liked to play football but I loved the jumping game, which was my favorite sport of all. Azeke and I would go to the nearest stream and try to jump from one side to the other while making sure we didn't fall in the water. If you could jump to the other side without getting wet, you won. If you lost, you had to face your mother; if I came home wet, my mother would scream at the top of her lungs.

But this is normal in the life of a boy, and overall, we lived a normal, comfortable life in Ethiopia. The UNHCR gave my mother enough money every month for food, rent, and other necessities. My mother also coordinated a special United Nations program to help refugee women by distributing food, clothes, and other goods. She took full responsibility of the distribution process.

I went to a public school in Addis because private schools were very expensive. My favorite teacher was Michael De Barton, my English teacher in the fifth grade. He was an American in his early twenties. As a child, I was very stubborn and only this American teacher in his early twenties knew how to deal with me, perhaps because he had been such a child himself. Mr. De Barton was as stubborn as I am; perhaps he was good with me because in his childhood, it was hard for teachers to deal with such a stubborn boy like him. There is nothing wrong with stubborn people; we just want people to give us a convincing argument. Most kids dislike school. They see school as pointless and they still don't value education. Mr. De Barton was understanding and patient. He knew that most of us didn't want to be there but he wanted us to make the best out of our school experience. Even though our teachers never laid a hand on me or any of the other students, Mr. De Barton was still special because he treated us as equals, not as children.

At the time, I wasn't very popular with my classmates because I always told the headmaster the truth when I was asked who started a fight. As a result, the ones who were to blame would be punished and in turn, they would punish me. The smarter children picked on the slower ones and I didn't like this because it was unfair. So I made some enemies, but I didn't care, because I only did what I thought was right. And I actually looked forward to school because I liked Mr. De Barton so much.

I discovered my passion for mathematics while I was in school in Ethiopia. All the other children hated math, while I enjoyed it. I learned to like numbers and calculations because of my math teacher, Mr. Butlet. He was Sudanese like me and he commanded great respect. When he came into the classroom, we all fell silent. He succeeded in making us pay attention, even though the majority of students hated math because he was very serious, but he was also very patient.

No one at school dared to call me a refugee or even mention my refugee status because the headmaster forbade it, but outside the classroom I was frequently reminded that I was not Ethiopian like them, but 'the other.' Once, I was talking to a girl I knew and a boy came up to us and said to her "Don't talk to him, he is just a refugee." For a sensitive child, this kind of treatment is hard to forget. Being a refugee was like a badge I was forced to wear, it became a part of my identity. At a certain point, I began to realize how this status made me helpless, in that there was nothing I could do to overcome it. As a refugee, I always felt that I wasn't good enough for anybody.

One day, a few years later, my mother told me we were moving to Nairobi. The Sudanese government had continued to harass refugees in Ethiopia, and since Sudan's largest opposition in the region happened to be the Kenyan government, Kenya became the hottest destination for refugees at the time. Kenya continued to play a very important role in bringing the Nairobi-based SPLM and the government together to negotiate peace agreements including the Comprehensive Peace Agreement (CPA), which was signed in Naivasha in June of 2005. In Nairobi, my father continued to work with the SPLA. He continued fighting in southern Sudan and I continued my academic journey. Education was my weapon of choice.

When we left Addis Ababa for Nairobi, I told Azeke we were going to come back. He thought he would see me again, so we didn't say our good-byes, and more than a decade later, I still miss him. I don't think I will ever forget him. We left Addis with very few possessions; refugees rarely have a lot of luggage. We took a car from Addis to Gambella in Western Ethiopia and, when we didn't find any means of transportation from Gambella to Nairobi, we walked for what seemed like an eternity but what was really only three days. We weren't walking alone though. We walked with many other families too. We didn't know any of them, but we had a lot in common. We were all refugees from different parts of East Africa and we all had a common destination—Nairobi.

Nairobi was Africa's 'little London.' This is how I liked to describe the city, even though I've never seen London. I thought it must resemble London because it has many skyscrapers. There are many schools and Kenyans dress and act the way I imagined Westerners would. Also, Nairobi and London have one important thing in common: rain. It rained a lot in Nairobi but instead of cleaning the city's dirty streets, rain made the city even dirtier. The more it rained the muddier and muddier it became and the more difficult it was to stay clean. If you happen to be in Nairobi and you see a Kenyan with dirty trousers, don't blame him, blame the weather.

In the 1990s, Kenyans used the term 'Nairobbery' to describe Nairobi's serious crime problem. Personally, I believe 'Nairobbery' is an accurate description. The city was very dangerous, even during the daytime. I avoided going out unless it was necessary because I didn't want to get mugged. When I did leave my home, I didn't carry much of value with me, and only took enough money for transportation. To survive *Nairobbery*, you had to be street-smart like me, and learn certain tricks, like putting your money in your socks. Unfortunately, I learned the hard way that the robbers learned that trick too, often making their victims remove their shoes and socks.

One of my good friends was walking along a Nairobi street and talking on his cell phone. All of a sudden, a man slapped him across the face, grabbed his phone, and ran away. It happened in less than a second and by the time my friend realized what had happened, the thief was gone. At night security was very tight; policemen stopped you to interrogate you and wanted to see your ID. It was easier to stay at home.

I spent most of my time indoors with my friend Atei, who was also a Sudanese refugee. We watched movies and we talked about everything from American movies, to rap music, to our future. Sometimes, we went to parties and gatherings held by refugees for refugees in our neighborhood, which was called Kentucky after the American state. There was nothing special about this area; it was simply another neighborhood in the large city. My father was making enough money from the SPLA to pay for our rent there, and my mother didn't have to work as she had in Addis Ababa.

After moving to Nairobi, my dad received a promotion. He made a good amount of money and our living conditions were much better. He was able to provide us with the necessities of a good life: shelter, food, warmth, water, and education. My father worked very hard to put me through school but university was out of the question. I had always wanted to go to Makerere University. It's Uganda's leading university and it was once called the Harvard of Africa. The list of Makerere's graduates include many of Africa's most prominent intellectuals, presidents, and authors such as Joseph Kabila, the current president of the Democratic Republic of the Congo, Oginga Odinga, the current vice president of Kenya, and Mahmood Mamdani, one of Africa's leading political scientists and professor of political science and anthropology at Colombia University.

Makerere was too expensive for me. At the time, I tried applying for scholarships, but all of them had an age limit and at sixteen, I was too young for any of them. My older siblings had graduated from high school, but they also couldn't afford to attend a university in Kenya. They both worked hard to save up money to continue their education, and I continued working hard on my studies at the Nakun high school. I loved my school and I continued pursuing my study of mathematics, which was still my passion. My math teacher at Nakun was a brilliant Kenyan man named Mr. Maro. He won his student's full attention with his unique style of teaching: every day he would come into the classroom and begin the lesson by telling a story. His stories were always about how men should live their lives. He always included the importance of math in his stories. He wholeheartedly believed that being good at math made you good at everything else. Being good at math makes you a good manager. A good manager is necessary for a successful business because you will also manage your finances and time very well. These are some of the things I learned from Mr. Maro.

When I was in tenth grade a miracle happened. I went to school only to find that we had a new teacher. When I saw him, I recognized him right away. From his look, I was sure he recognized me as well. He surprised me with a big warm hug. Mr. Michael De Barton was now teaching in Nairobi. After finding Mr. De Barton again, I knew that miracles happen when you least expect it.

Because Kenya was very close to my original home in Yirol, south Sudan, we were able to visit our friends and family once a year. Yirol is a beautiful place, very green, with many streams. The people in Yirol hail from my tribe, the Dinka, who are the largest tribe in south Sudan, and are considered to be very intelligent. The ambassador of southern Sudan to Egypt is a Dinka from Yirol. We have a reputation of being very wise people. We were fortunate to be able to return home occasionally; some refugees leave their land without knowing if and when they will return. We would leave in November and sometimes stay until February, when we would return to Nairobi so I could go back to school. At that time the war raged in southern Sudan, but we made our annual visits regardless, and survived with our people. Even if we could stay for only a short period of time, it was very important to my family that we return to Yirol to suffer with our tribesmen and go through whatever they went through. We could not simply abandon our friends and family, and come back when the area is at peace.

At sixteen I was old enough to understand a lot more about the nature of the war in the south. I started blaming God for it. I blamed Him for the war mainly because I was displaced and a refugee as a result of it. I had always felt that being a refugee took away my dignity. Now I began to feel it more and more. We prayed to God to help us, and to stop the war, but it never came to an end. God seemed to have abandoned Sudan and Africa. Africans saw each other as the enemy, and turned on their own brothers. The truth is that only peace is going to save us, and this peace is going to come from within, from Africa itself, from each individual African. This is something Africans need to understand: that they cannot expect to do nothing and wait for others to save them.

Like other guys my age, I started trying my luck with girls as I grew up. But there was a serious impediment in all of my relationships with women, namely my father. He thought girls were going to distract me from my studies, so he made sure I stayed away from them. My sister was his accomplice and his number one spy. Whenever I went out with a girl, she would find out and tell him. And he would always punish me.

I lived in Nairobi for nine years, until I graduated from high school, and then I decided to go home. Home, of course, was Sudan. It was 2000 and I was very ready to go. Even though I'd never really lived full time in Sudan, I still felt it was my home. I belonged there. I chose to go back to Khartoum because the south was still unsafe and underdeveloped. Khartoum, the capital, had better infrastructure, and I thought I could feel as much at home there as I would in the south. I didn't know what to expect at the time, but I took my chances.

Nothing could have prepared me for the surprise I received at the Khartoum airport. Let's just say I never made it to Khartoum. Airport security tore up my papers and accused me of being an SPLM soldier. There was so much tension between the SPLM and the government, that the government and the SPLM considered each other to be terrorist organizations. I was surprised when they accused me of being part of the SPLM, because they had no evidence to support that. I was wearing a necklace with the southern Sudan flag on it, which was also associated with the SPLM. I didn't think this matter was serious at the time and I didn't think a necklace would cause so many problems. But as a result, I didn't get into Khartoum that night, and instead I was sent on the next plane back to Nairobi.

I stayed in Nairobi for another three years because I didn't have the qualifications and the necessary permit to get a proper job. I stayed home and indulged in one of my favorite pastimes—reading. I read history books and biographies. I remember one of my favorite books was about Charlie Chaplin. I also went back to my high school passion—math. I solved many math problems in those years, and I also worked as an unpaid tutor for my younger siblings.

The three years I spent after my forced return from Khartoum passed quickly. In 2003, I was ready to go back to Khartoum. The experience is not for the faint-hearted, but I remained hopeful. I stood at Khartoum International Airport in 2003 with no ability to communicate to the airport official who stood in front of me. In 2003, Sudan lacked national coherence. We didn't have a lingua franca. I couldn't speak Arabic and the official spoke only Arabic. I responded in English. This language barrier kept us from making any progress.

But somehow, I was allowed into my country's capital. I was expecting some serious accusations at the airport. I wondered if, in 2000, they had written down my name on a blacklist or if they vowed to ban me from Khartoum for life. I wasn't guilty of anything but in Sudan you are guilty until you are formally accused of being guilty. Then, if you are found guilty, you're in serious trouble and sometimes you're in serious trouble even if you aren't.

What I hated most about Khartoum was the weather. It was suffocating. There are no words to describe how hot it is. Before going to Khartoum, my father gave me money for rent and other necessities, and I rented a house in al-Khalaka, Juba, a neighborhood south of Khartoum. I didn't know anyone there, but people were kind to me. One day, while I was looking for a job, I saw an advertisement for a teaching position at a church. I immediately applied and was hired to teach Catholic studies to students who, unbeknownst to me, were both Christian and Muslim. I didn't know or care that my students included Muslims, but Sudanese security officials cared very much.

One day, they came to the church when I was in class, knocked on the door and asked me to step outside. They said one of students' fathers complained that I was trying to convert his daughter. The little girl came with her friends and she probably didn't know there was anything wrong with learning about another religion. I was told that after today, they would be watching me, and if they saw any Muslim students, I would be jailed.

The actions of the security men seemed to make sure the Sudanese people stayed divided and not united. If we are united, we are going to be strong. Before that, I didn't judge people based on their religion, but sadly, this incident opened my eyes to our differences. After that, I didn't feel good about what I was doing anymore. This incident marked the end of my visit to Khartoum.

For years, my aunt had asked me to join her in Australia where she had resettled. I never took her request into consideration, but after the problem with the security men, I decided to take her up on it. There was no Australian embassy in Sudan, so I had to travel to Egypt and apply for an Australian visa from there. I took a train from Khartoum to Halfa, a city in north Sudan, and from Halfa I took a ferry to Aswan, then I took a bus from Aswan to

Cairo. This journey took five days, but I didn't complain since a plane was out of the question. If I dared to enter Cairo by plane, security would no doubt accuse me of being an SPLM soldier again, and they might arrest me. Refugees don't take planes, they take journeys.

When I reached Cairo, I was utterly lost. I just kept thinking of Nairobi, I wanted to go back to Nairobi more than anything in the world. Cairo was the most hard-to-understand chaos I have ever seen. It was huge and crowded. I don't know enough words to explain the human traffic in places such as Ain Shams.

The most distressing thing for me was how I was viewed. People kept staring at me. I felt weird and scared. They made me feel like a walking problem. I didn't understand why they stared at me like that, I wasn't a danger to Egypt and I wasn't an impediment to the development of the Egyptian society or economy. My uncle's wife, who was there at the time, picked me up from the bus station. I lived with her in Zeitoun for eight months. After that, I went to live with my aunt in Kubri al-Qubba.

I wasn't looking forward to living in Cairo. I despised the instability in my life caused by moving from one city to another. I wanted to stay in one place and settle down, and Australia seemed so appealing. My grandmother sent me a lot of pictures of Melbourne, where she lives, and other places in Australia. As soon as I reached Cairo, I went to the Australian embassy and applied for an immigration visa for Australia. I didn't expect the process to take a long time, but they asked for many papers to be filled out, signed, and stamped.

The first time I applied for an immigration visa, I wasn't as lucky as my mother fondly imagined me to be. My visa was denied even though I gave them all the papers they needed. After the Comprehensive Peace Agreement (CPA) was signed in 2005, all the embassies stopped resettling Sudanese refugees because it was now considered safe to return back to south Sudan. Some refugees returned to south Sudan, but I didn't want to go back.

After my papers were denied, I became deeply depressed. Life in Egypt is hard. Egyptians like to joke about everything and everyone. People talk to me in a condescending way because of my skin color. I get a lot of stares and I get called some very unpleasant names when I'm walking in the streets. I remember once a man insulted me and by then, I was so fed up with everything, I told him to leave me alone. He and his friends kept laughing at me and I told them I didn't want to hear anymore jokes. I started arguing with one of them, but all of a sudden, at least ten men came running up and began to attack me. I was beaten badly. They had knives with them and they started cutting me. One of them cut me in my thigh and it was bleeding uncontrollably. I was taken to a hospital, where the wound required stitches. In my twenty-three years, it was the first time I had been in a fight like that. I felt very much alone because the man who attacked me had so many loyal friends helping him and I had no one on my side. I have never felt so alone.

Just as I thought my luck was gone, I met Susan, a lawyer from Australia. She was interested in my case and told me she would help me. I'm convinced now that I'm going to go to Australia in 2009, because she wouldn't tell me she could help me if she couldn't. Next year, I'm going to be in Australia, and it's not going to be like Cairo. Australia is like a dream. When I talk to my family on the phone, they tell me it's so beautiful and organized. They have good universities and the living standards are very high. I'm going to go to one of the universities, because I've never had the opportunity to do my undergraduate studies. Education is the most important thing to me; it's mainly why I want to go to Australia. Through my church, I met a physiology professor at Flinders University. They have an excellent science engineering program at Flinders, and she told me she is going to help me get into the university. It's very easy for refugees to get into universities in Australia. The government provides refugees with a lot of education opportunities.

My dream is to get a bachelor's degree and eventually to get a PhD in chemical engineering, so if war ever breaks out again, I will be able to make weapons and demand my rights. I will always demand my rights and my land. This is why the SPLM took up arms; they demanded rights for the southern Sudanese people and they wanted federalism in the south and democracy in all of Sudan. Sometimes, having weapons can help make your voice heard. People listen to you when you ask for your rights. To bring peace, we need freedom of speech. We must have essential rights, including the right to live.

But who will bring freedom to Sudan? Nobody knows. I'm for the independence of the south. In 2011, I'm voting yes. Yes, for independence that is. If the living conditions improve in the south, if the peace process is fully implemented, we could have a united Sudan, but now, a divided Sudan seems like a more appealing idea.

Here in Cairo, I'm trying to make the best out of it. I work at three clinics. Before I started working at the clinics, I attended a month long training course aimed at health workers. When mothers bring their babies to the clinics I work at, I give them a check-up to see if their condition is serious enough to send them to an Egyptian doctor in Zamalek.

It takes three jobs to keep me occupied, but nothing keeps me from rapping, something I really love. Every time I rap, I also use my own voice to make beats. I can't sing, but when I rap, I'm really good at it. My favorite song of all time is "It Wasn't Me" by Shaggy. I really like his style, he is a good rapper. Also, "Riding Dirty," one of Chamillionaire's best songs, is amazing. In 2007, he won a Grammy award for the best rap song of the year. He is my favorite rapper. I can't tell you how inspired I am by rappers like Chamillionaire. Born to Nigerian parents in Washington, DC, he is now one of the most popular rappers. This August, I'm going to free-style with a friend of mine at a jam we've been organizing for a while. This is what inspires me to get up every day.

Mariette

Soraya Samir Gaafar

I was born in 1967 in the city of Juba, and lived there until I was twenty, when the war came. My early memories of Juba are happy ones. My father had a good job as a government administrator for the Department of Utilities. His salary was sufficient to provide his wife and four children with everything we could possible need. We had a big house in one of the nicest neighborhoods. I remember this house as enormous, having many rooms including a separate dining room, which was a sign of affluence in Juba at that time. Some of my happiest memories took place in the back yard where we—my two older brothers and my youngest sister—used to play. When my father was not working, he took us on trips to visit our relatives, who lived in the Juba area, and to the banks of the Nile, where my brothers taught me to swim. Sometimes we took the ferry to the island of Rajaf, where we'd bring a picnic of beef, and light a fire to build a barbecue out of rocks and wire; we ate grilled meat with bread, pumpkin, and spinach, and we used the fire to heat water for tea.

One of the benefits that my father received as a government administrator was a company car, and we used it on weekends after church. Sometimes we went to Yay, a two-day drive, to visit cousins, aunts, and uncles. Juba at that time, in the early 1970s, was a beautiful place where it seemed we could find everything we needed. The markets sold plenty of fresh meats, fruit, and vegetables and we loved a special Sudanese dish made of ground peanuts and *lubya*, black-eyed beans. We felt free then, and safe, knowing my father could take care of us and get us everything we needed. He was the kind of man who knew how to be happy, and that made everyone around him happy too. We were such a close family and I loved every minute of the time I spent with him. We thought that our safe, protected lives and our happiness as a close family would last forever. Little did we know that that would soon change.

My parents wanted their children to get a good education, so at six years old I was enrolled in one of the better private schools. It was an all-girls school and it was expensive, but my father could afford it and he wanted the best for his children. My favorite subjects were art and reading. I remember very little from that time except how happy I was. It rained often in Juba, which is why the land is so green, and as soon as the rain would start, my friends and I would run outside to play and get wet. At night my mother would sing us songs and tell us stories; I wish I could remember them, to tell to my own children, but I've forgotten them, and only recall that they were soothing.

This happy life came to an end when my father died suddenly, after three days of a common illness. His pension was small and we struggled to survive. Soon we couldn't afford our school fees, and I was enrolled in a new school that I didn't like at all. It was a mix of boys and girls and there were no school supplies, not even paper, so we had to write on the floor. The teachers taught one viewpoint and did not welcome ideas or imagination. Sometimes they hit us, but at least they were fair and did not discriminate between boys and girls. My younger sister hated school so much, she cried every day.

We had to leave our big house and move into a two-room apartment in a military barracks. It had no garden but there was a dirt playground nearby. My mother took a job cleaning offices and she worked hard to support her four children. My dream as a child was to continue my education because, despite the limitations of my school, I loved learning. Even though my brothers teased me and told me I didn't know anything, when I had an exam, they would help me study. My goal then was to be a healthcare worker.

My mother wanted us to fulfill our dreams. While we got some support from our church, she also managed to make a little extra money selling sweets at the market. She made small, round waffles that are dipped in red syrup to raise money to pay the bills. This extra money was especially helpful when my brother fell from a tree and broke his leg. But by the time I was fourteen there just wasn't enough money anymore. One of my brothers was in the university then, and he had to leave. I quit school and stayed home to help my mother make *sambusas*, salty pies filled with meat or cheese, to sell at the market. My sister, who was then ten, decided that she wanted to live with our cousins in the country, closer to children her own age, and work with them in the fields. At first we missed each other very much but, because we visited these cousins often, we ended up seeing her almost every week.

And my sad life continued. I wanted very much to go to college and knew I could not afford it. I always felt inferior, not only about not going to college, but because my friends' fathers bought for them clothes, shoes, and jewelry that I could never have. I began to make a little extra money sewing; I crocheted tablecloths and baby socks, which I sold in a local store. This store offered free lessons to local girls and then took their better pieces on consignment and gave them 50 percent of the profit, which we felt was fair since they provided all the supplies. But when I got paid, I gave half my fee to my mother, and with the rest bought my own needles and thread so that I could make new pieces, sell them on my own, and get all the profits.

Men in Sudan at that time were very well behaved and there was no such thing as sexual harassment or inappropriate behavior. When I fell in love for the first time, it was with a man outside my tribe and I was devastated because my mother would not allow me to marry him; I am Bari, and my prospective fiancé was a Dinka. My mother rejected him and at age nineteen, I married a Bari man who asked my mother for my hand. It was not an arranged marriage. I knew him from church and from the neighborhood and, although he was not my first love, I learned to accept and love him. He had a good job as a driver, and he bought me nice dresses, which I appreciated. When we married, I moved into his house with his brother, which was a change for me, as I'd always lived with my mother, but I accepted it because it is a tradition for a bride to leave her parents—and I saw my mother often. In 1985, I had a daughter and we became a very happy family.

My life changed dramatically once more when civil war broke out and we moved to Khartoum. The stress of the war and being so far from home took a toll on me. The first sign of war in Juba was the presence of soldiers with guns, of death on the streets. We'd all hide under the beds when we heard gunfire, and anyone unlucky enough to be outside in plain view risked being shot. My 15-year-old cousin was killed while she was walking down the street. And we didn't even know what this war was about! We'd dig holes to hide in because sometimes the soldiers would keep firing into a house and you were only safe under the ground. There was a food crisis, prices rose, and the noise of gunshots kept us awake. We had little or no electricity; I remember a roomful of people sitting around one little lamp. And the soldiers used to hit women, which surprised me because most Sudanese men I'd known were polite.

It was too dangerous to remain in Juba; I feared they would take my husband to fight in the battlefields. We had to go to Khartoum, where no one felt the impact of the war. But it was very hard to leave Juba for Khartoum; there were no trains and to make the trip by car or bus could take many days, not to mention the danger on the road. Security police could stop your vehicle, make you get out, and beat you up—or take the men hostage and force them to fight in the war. Flying was the only option and it was expensive. But we had friends in the military who arranged for us—my family and my husband's 13-year-old brother—to fly in a government plane.

Khartoum was a surprise; it was a very modern city, and in comparison the only city I'd known seemed like a suburb. At first it was frightening, the skyline intimidated me, but in two weeks I felt very comfortable and familiar there. My husband's family had a house downtown that was large but which became crowded after we arrived. I was not comfortable there; I felt I was imposing on his family, taking up their space. I quickly found work as a cook and housekeeper for the Nigerian ambassador and for a doctor's wife, motivated by the thought of earning enough money to get our own home. My husband worked as a supplier for school administrators and also as a truck driver transporting oil, fruit, and vegetables. Sometimes he would be gone for as long as three weeks. In six months, we were able to rent our own two-bedroom apartment and my husband's sister came to stay with us, which made it easier for me when my husband was away for work.

Our ground floor apartment had access to a large garden and I used to play with my daughter there. Those were happy times. I had four more children and because my husband was doing well enough financially, we were able to build a one-story house in the same neighborhood with a yard big enough to raise goats and chickens. We built enough rooms for everyone, including my sister-in-law and her two children. I got a job as a kindergarten teacher in a private school, and we remained there for the next thirteen years.

Religious oppression forced us to leave Sudan in 2004. The school where I taught accused me of trying to convert the students, some of whom were Muslim. I was forced to work on Sundays, so I couldn't go to church and I was afraid that the school officials, who were becoming threatening, would take drastic measures and fire me or hit me. Once, walking home from school, a car stopped and I was pulled inside, blindfolded, and taken to an unfamiliar room and tied up. Men whose voices I did not recognize accused me of trying to convert the Muslim children to Christianity. I was beaten when I pleaded my innocence. I remained a prisoner for three days during which I was given only one sandwich and a little water. Then I was taken back to the car and dropped off along a highway. I knew, then, I had to leave Sudan. My husband would at first remain and then follow me. I'd heard that in Egypt it was possible to get a job, own property, and have a good life and so I decided to take my children to Cairo. I had to be careful because if anyone knew we were leaving, word would spread and the government authorities would find us and make us return. I couldn't even tell my children, who were three, seven, twelve, and eighteen at the time, for fear they might tell their friends.

I can never forget the night we had to sneak out of our house in the dark of night to catch a train that would take us to Halfa. From Halfa we would take a boat that would ferry us across the Aswan dam to the train station, where we would catch a train that would take us to Cairo. My heart trembled with fear throughout the journey. I was terrified that someone would recognize us, that I'd be interrogated and arrested, and taken from my children. But nothing like that happened. My husband's relatives met us at the train station, took us to their home in Dirmilag, and my husband joined us.

The day we arrived in Cairo, exhausted as I was, I went immediately to the UNHCR and applied for refugee status. I was sure someone would find out we were illegal aliens and send us back to Sudan, and although we got the status in three months, the anxiety and fear I experienced made it feel like three years. I quickly found work as a housekeeper in Nasr City and my husband took odd jobs when he could get them. But even with our salaries life was hard. Our relatives lived in a two-room apartment and it was so crowded that the boys sometimes slept in the reception area. Until we received refugee status, my children did not go to school and spent their time at home playing and watching TV, which made the house feel even more crowded.

As soon as our status came through, three of my children were enrolled at a church school in Abbasiya, and my son went to an Egyptian English language school called Mataria. Later, I transferred all my children to Mataria. One of my sons was kicked out of school because he was involved in a fight on campus. The children at school pick fights with those who are different. If an outsider comes into their area, they take drastic measures that extend to heavy beating. My son, who is now 18 years old, takes courses at Kanasia, which is part of a church. My husband and I found an apartment in Hadayeq al-Zeitoun, but we didn't stay there long. One night soon after we moved in, two Egyptian men came inside through the balcony while we were sleeping, carrying knives. I don't know if they wanted to kill us or steal from us. My daughter opened the apartment door and screamed down the staircase for help. The owner of the flat and other residents of our building woke up and directly came to our house. They were of tremendous help. We trapped the thieves inside our apartment so that they would not escape. The building owner, my daughter, and I took the men to the police station where we filed an official complaint. Despite the fact that we turned them in, I was terrified and I insisted on finding a new apartment after that, with more secure doors and windows. I needed to feel safe. And now I do.

Life here has been good despite the hardships, which come mainly in the form of racist comments and more physical forms of harassment. Walking down the street, I hear men shout "soda," which means 'black.' They find it very funny to push their friends in front of us so that we collide with a sudden jolt and feel the pressure of a strange body against us. They laugh and laugh at our surprised faces. They even throw rocks at us in the poorer neighborhoods and young Egyptian men do not hesitate to touch young African women, to grab at their breasts. A woman I know opened her door when a man claiming to be an electrician knocked; he said he wanted to read her meter. He entered the house, saw she was alone, and raped her violently. And of course, there is nothing the women can do about it.

To complain to an official is not only a waste of time but would only bring more trouble. A woman who goes to the police, claiming to have been raped can become even more vulnerable, accused of being a prostitute. She can go to jail, endure beatings, or more indignities in the police station. In the upscale areas like Nasr City, Maadi, and Zamalek, Egyptians have more respect for themselves and for us, and we rarely experience any harm there.

But we face some form of discrimination every time we walk on the streets in Cairo. There is not a day that goes by that this harassment does not occur. Still, life here is better than in Sudan in terms of providing for the family. And our children are safe, which is what matters most.

My days are busy, so perhaps I do not suffer because I have no time to be unhappy. I get up at 6am and because I don't like to eat breakfast, I have a little extra time to prepare clean school uniforms for my children. They have breakfast at school, so I drop them off at 7am and take the metro to Maadi, where I teach at St. Joseph's School. I work from 8am to 2pm, six days a week and I make LE 450 per month. By the time I get home, it is about 3:30 or 4pm and I prepare dinner. My children, who will have been home alone since 1pm, are usually busy with homework or games. Three days a week I go to English classes in Ain Shams from 5 to 8:30pm; the course costs only LE 50 and is helping me improve my language skills, so I try to go regularly. By the time I get home, it's after 9pm and I do housework and laundry until midnight, when I am grateful to climb into bed. My husband leaves for work early in the morning and returns at 8pm, so he spends time with the children in the evening while I'm at my class. And the children have a schedule too; their school—the Sacred Heart—has a strong social program with sports activities that keeps them busy three days a week after school.

I cannot say I am unhappy in Egypt but when I am sure that the war is over and that all religious discrimination has ended, I want to return home to Sudan. I miss my mother and my brothers, who still live in Juba, very much and I want them to come and visit but of course they cannot. It is expensive and difficult, considering that we have been granted asylum. I wish I could go back to Sudan in order to work there and build a house of our own. I want my children to go back so that they can experience their home culture, and can learn about their traditions without being made fun of. I wish that my children would get married and have children so I can be a happy grandmother.

If our situation had not turned out to be this way, I would have wanted to open a school for children in Sudan in order to teach them ethics and direct them to the right path. I have always been good at passing on good ideas and advice to people, and I love to help as well. And I am grateful for the asylum that Egypt has given us. Not all Egyptians have treated me badly. I worked for a family for a short while. They provided me with clothes for my children and sometimes even presents. Even after I left my work there, they still keep in contact with me by calling me often. I would like to say to all helpful Egyptians "May God fulfill all your wishes." But Sudan will always be my home. It is a part of me and, one day, I hope to return there.

Ali

Ali Atef
Karim Higazy

Honestly, I had not told my children. They were completely in the dark about why they were ripped away from their country, the reason we had left our home in Sudan so suddenly. "We're going to Egypt for the holidays," was the fabrication we used to comfort them and to keep them in that state of oblivion to protect them from the harsher reality my wife and I were facing—the same reality that I often saw driving my wife to tears time and time again. I knew they could at least salvage what could well be described as something of a happy childhood if they were shielded from the forces that drove us from Sudan. By taking them to the zoo and buying them candy as much as I could, I attempted to reinforce that youthful happiness, to compensate for what they were deprived of.

I had often contemplated how long I should keep the truth from them. When would I truthfully answer those tough, crucial questions they would throw at me, interrogating me with those youthful, intelligent eyes, hungry for any shred of justification to explain why we weren't enjoying our house in Sudan, the real reason we weren't home. I consulted a friend, who told me that I should tell them the truth, hoping for the best. "I tossed and turned all night, I could not sleep.... I was up wondering if I'd given you the right advice," were her first words the next time we met. I proceeded to tell her how it went. I explained how I first sat them down and told them the story. They had taken it in with maturity, to the point where a bit of role reversal took place and I found myself on the receiving end of a lecture about honesty. "If you always taught us about honesty and that we should not lie, yet you're here telling us that you lied to us ... then what exactly are we supposed to do?"

That's when the interrogation began, and the tough questions bombarded me one by one. They asked me why I had left Sudan. I answered their question, as if in introspection, telling them that in Sudan I was opposed to the government, which didn't allow people proper education and enough medicine. Because I was opposed to the government, they wanted to get rid of me. To my luck, my children agreed with me that my demands were normal and that everyone should have access to education and medicine.

It was a relief in many ways to have told my children the truth and they even began to play a part when it came to economizing. They asked for money less frequently, and they came to terms with our tough situation. Nevertheless, there still remains that lingering concern regarding my children's living conditions. When we'd first arrived, we found a tiny apartment (about eight square meters) in Misr al-Gadida, which was a far cry from our big house in Kordofan, which was about 250 square meters.

My children got used to the small space but I wasn't able to let them go outside the house too much, fearing that due to their youth, they wouldn't understand their surroundings. Now they're a little older. They can go to the supermarket or to the stores close by. The small confined nature of our living quarters was causing my children to develop all sorts of problems and disorders. One of my sons began to display signs of an attention disorder and memory problems. That's why I encouraged their trips to the supermarket—not only did it make them happy, it helped me instill independence in them.

I often reflect on the troubled past I had kept from my children. I used to work as an operations manager at the airport in Kordofan. I had decided to open my own transport company—both air and road routes. It was easy to start since I knew everybody who was working in the field. But, as an operations manager, I was arrested twice. The government suspected I was smuggling medicine and food to the rebels in the south. The second time they saw that I sent shipments to churches in the south, I was arrested, and accused of working against the government. I was actually allowing shipments to go down to the south to the NGOs and multi-donor agencies working there because they had no other way to get supplies. I signed off on the cargo shipments. To the police, my signature meant that I was supporting the rebels in the south.

It was the night we decided to leave Kordofan for Khartoum and then Egypt that the police came to arrest me for the third time. At that time, I was an independent operations manager. I had sent a shipment of medicine that would be delivered to Darfur. On the way, however, the car was hijacked by rebel groups. Policing was conducted to confirm this and I got the news. The police forces followed the rebels, saw the shipments they had intercepted, and saw my name on the shipments. This time they came to me and informed me that there was no way I could disprove that I was in fact helping the rebels. They arrested me and I was sent to prison.

In prison, political prisoners are treated worse than anyone else. The night guards especially would treat us horribly. They would come and use our arms as ashtrays. Another method of torture and labor was their forcing us to carry piles of stones from one area to another. It's not something I like to recall or tell, and it definitely was not a pleasant experience. Luckily, my friends who had connections were able to get me transferred to a military hospital that was right next to the airport. I planned to escape from the hospital, take a plane to Khartoum to meet my family (who were already there waiting for me), and then take a plane to Cairo. From the military hospital, I was able to enter the airport easily, and since no one knew of my arrest, I was met with the kindness and courtesy I had become accustomed to. I boarded the plane to Khartoum and arrived there in a couple of hours.

The police were definitely not happy about my escape. They interrogated and tortured my youngest brother to find a way to get to me. In response, my friends concocted a rumor that I had gone to the south. And so, while the police were searching for me in the south, I stayed in Khartoum for two weeks planning our departure to Cairo.

I guess I am now officially categorized as a refugee. Being a refugee is a status on paper for the authorities, so that the government can work with individuals and deal with them on a legal level. This is what brought about the 1951 Convention on the Status of Refugees. Police officers don't understand the form we carry, nor do they know that the right refugee documents do not allow deportation, according to the government-signed agreement. Strictly speaking, refugees are defined by their border-crossing, from one country's border to another.

The idea of having refugees within the country is not as bad as the host citizens may think. Refugees occasionally benefit the economy—they're not just poor people coming to steal Egyptian citizens' opportunities. They're here because they have problems. Honestly, I feel Egyptians should muster a sense of pride as a result of our need for their help. Since we come here, it must mean that we feel that Egypt is secure, that there are commonalities between us. The term refugee is one that applies to everyone because when you, for example, switch from seeking your mother's protection to your father's, you are also a refugee and in that sense I have no problem with the movement implied within the term. I went from one insecure place to another. That's what makes you a refugee: when you cross borders. Otherwise, I would be an internally displaced person. I feel bad for my nation; I swing between feelings of guilt and failure, mostly because I ended up leaving people who are dependent on me and leaving a job that I feel helped people.

There are many cases of refugees forsaking their newfound sanctuary. However, people who go back to Sudan are usually simple. Most of the time it boils down to people who weren't able to live with the Egyptians, whether that be because of language, education, or racial barriers. Sometimes, the uneducated refugees act in unacceptable ways. But if you've lived in forests your whole life, the modern spaces seem so different to you. The forest is yours and in your forest, space is abundant. A bathroom could be five hundred meters, and the space can accommodate huge families up to twenty-five people. This becomes a problem when you come to an urban place, such as Cairo.

As much as I appreciate my refuge here, I have to admit, leaving my country was very difficult; especially since I knew top confidential information regarding the military. I often torture myself with the notion that, while I was given the opportunity to leave, people there are still living in hell. One thing that I learned through my education, is recognizing your rights and those of other people's. If the people in the village are given the chance to be educated, they will be able to get their rights. This is one of the two problems I see in Sudan: education, because there aren't enough schools, and health, because healthcare in Sudan is insufficient.

Private schools are growing, while government schools still have people sitting on the ground without any roofs. The government's high-ranking jobs are given to certain tribes, meaning that if you're not from the Halla or Dumbula tribe, you won't get certain posts. Certain people have access to improvement but the rest are considered oppositionists and because the government owns most of the sectors, they're not given much of a chance. I have hoped to change these conditions since I was a student.

Just one detrimental factor to educational reform, for example, is the fact that government teachers don't get their salaries on time . . . not that they even get high salaries or anything. Also, if a teacher shows any kind of antagonism toward the government, it is likely the government will clamp down on him or her. For any kind of political success, the government has to respect the people and their culture—that would solve half the problem. Here's a peculiar aspect of the south Sudan culture: if you don't dance with the people, it means you don't like them. Now, the government should know that!

Anyway, I realize that, so far, I've been discussing my problems and political views but I have not shared my background. I come from the Kordofan region, 625 kilometers from Khartoum, the capital of Sudan—a place I've come to call home, with its unique customs and norms. In Kordofan, people take their shoes off when they come into someone else's house, and they bend toward you to signal a warm hello. This is the traditional custom.

You would probably never get bored living there; there are strange happenings every day. I can even recall one story involving a girl who had to marry her cousin. When she was in the market one day, a man noticed her and recited some lines of poetry to her—an event she reported to her mother excitedly. When the cousin overheard her, he went and killed this man. So the brother of the man went to kill the murderer ... and he did. It was a one-to-one approach, and it kept happening until there were seven people dead on each side. The Ministry of the Interior sent police forces to stop the honor killings. Both tribes came together to fight the police. The minister had to withdraw the police forces to avoid more killings. The death toll in the end reached two-hundred people. The woman should've just kept her mouth shut.

But, I digress. In Kordofan, I live in the north, in a city called Abyad, near the international airport. In Abyad, we're famous for our crops and we're known for being the center of many non-governmental organizations and multi-donor agencies. That being the case, we also have many foreigners that live and work in the area from all different kinds of organizations: WFP, UNICEF, FAO, SCF,[8] Sudan Aid, and Oxfam, being a few of them. Because of the easy road access and air routes to the area, we have many private organizations that have set up shop there as well. The Catholic Church has established organizations there, as well as Norwegian Aid. There are some governmental church organizations as well as organizations funded by the Kingdom of Saudi Arabia. It's a pretty stable area that has easy access to air routes so that the cargo that comes from these organizations lands there safely. Beforehand, it used to be carried by military airplanes that were imported from Russia (as opposed to from the US, a country Sudan had problems with at the time). These NGOs have been here for some time. Most of them came in around 1988 when there was a big drought that affected Sudan. Actually, that is when Michael Jackson also recorded the single "We are the World," which everyone in Sudan can probably sing along to. I even have it as my cell phone ring tone.

Around 1988, I was about to graduate from Comboni College in Abyad. I had decided to head up to Khartoum and major in political science at Khartoum University. To me, having a degree in political science was very important considering the nature of the country. I studied foreign policy. Funnily enough, I met my wife in university.

How I met my wife is actually a very interesting story. We both went to university together and initially hated each other. I thought she was spoiled; she thought I was full of it. We both purposefully avoided each other. We graduated with minimal communication and I thought that would be the end of it. A couple of years later, when I got hired at an aviation company as the head of accounting, she came into the room, looked up at me, and we both ignored each other. We decided that we'd work on a strictly professional basis and that would be it. At the time, I had a Syrian girlfriend who was also Christian. One time, I asked my wife whether she thought a marriage between a Muslim and a Christian would work out, to which she responded: if both of you have a will then it should be fine. A couple of months later, however, I broke up with my Syrian girlfriend and started to realize that I had feelings for this colleague of mine. One day while we were working together, I asked her the same question I had asked a few months before: would it work out between a Muslim and a Christian, if she were in this position? She looked straight at me and answered "yes." I had to talk to her sister to know how to approach the family. I could not go to the father, because he would undoubtedly refuse, and it would be quite a scandal.

We decided to get married on our own. We went to the marriage courts and, through my connections, were able to complete the papers without going through the bureaucracy of obtaining the father's consent. Usually, the father of the bride is sought out at least two days before the marriage and asked for his approval. My wife's father, however, was politely informed of the marriage only thirty minutes before the legal papers were signed. We had a big wedding and everyone came—even, to our pleasure, my wife's family.

Now we have three children, who, I'm sure will someday drive me crazy with their inquisitive questions. At this moment, they're interested in learning where babies come from. They're at that stage. Their mother explained that you'd have to go the pharmacy, get some pills, take them, and then wait for the baby to grow. So for the past several weeks, they've been monitoring how many pills she takes, and calculating the number of babies she'll be expecting.

My daughter, in fact, does not stop asking embarrassing questions. One time, we were visiting a couple who had just had a baby. The baby had been born with only one ear, so I warned my daughter not to ask any questions. So, she went inside to play with the other children. All was good. Then she came out and politely asked, "Auntie, if the baby grows up and has weak eyesight, what will you do?" And, of course, the mother responded, "Why, we'd get him glasses."

"But how would he wear them?" she asked. I almost died.

Now I work as an interpreter at the UNHCR. I go to work every day and realize just how hard Egyptians find it to accept refugees. It's sad.

I plan to go to the US. I just had an interview at the US embassy—after my three years in Cairo—to apply as an asylum-seeker.

I requested that my wife and kids be kept in another room while I was asked questions, because I didn't want them to hear everything that had happened to me. I didn't want my wife to relive the experiences. About a week later, they informed me that our application had been approved.

When I go to the United States, I want to create awareness amongst people—both those living in the US and those living back home in Sudan. I want people to know their rights, to respect others, and to appreciate what they have.

These are but my views.

Mishca

Olivia Bishara

I was born in Juba, the capital of southern Sudan, six years before the war began. I remember my family's big four-story house surrounded by a large garden full of tall trees. I used to spend most of my time as a young child in the garden, running and playing with my sisters and brothers. My brothers used to climb the trees; the lush greenery made a perfect place to play. The garden was my favorite place but I also loved the rooftop terrace on the top floor of our house. I remember how much I loved to stand on the rooftop when I was only four years old and from my vantage point, the garden appeared to stretch endlessly into the distance. Then my mother would call me downstairs to have breakfast with my sisters and brothers.

My family was a large one, and my life was simple and happy. I had eight sisters and six brothers. Each one of my siblings had unique characteristics that made them special, and, for my younger brother, it was kindness. I was closest to my two youngest brothers and two eldest sisters, with whom I used to play and share secrets. We would wake up early in the morning and go downstairs to have our breakfast at the children's table. It is a Sudanese custom that the elders and youngsters eat separately. Dad used to have breakfast with my uncle while my sisters, brothers, and I would have our meals together. This helped us become independent, since we ate without our mother from a young age. After breakfast, we would spend all morning and afternoon playing together in our enormous garden. I used to love to play hide and seek, because our big house offered so many hiding places in the many cupboards and under the beds. Once, while we were playing, my older sister fell asleep in the cupboard she was hiding in and we spent two hours looking for her.

My father was the Minister of the Upper Nile, Equatoria, and Bahr Ghazal, which gave him many diverse responsibilities; he had to guarantee the security and safety of the police and governmental employees and also to make sure that everyone was doing his job efficiently. He was referred to as "the eye of the government," and he commanded such a good income for the family that my mother did not have to work. Her only job was to stay at home with us and to take care of everything concerning our lives.

Our family, as is common in the south, is Christian. My father was first taught about Christianity in school and once he became a Christian, the rest of my family followed suit. Still, religion was separate from some Sudanese traditions; many men who considered themselves to be good Christians had multiple wives, a practice that is not sanctioned by the Bible.

My mother had a great influence on us and we played a game in which we copied the way she cooked by putting vegetables, onions, and spaghetti together to make meals for our family of dolls to eat. We set a small fire in the garden using wood that we gathered, and we cooked over it, which was dangerous since we were so young. My mother used to shout at us to put out the fire but we enjoyed the game so much that we played it almost every day. Bedtime was early, at seven, because my mother believed this was best. She was a strong woman who encouraged us to study hard and always wanted us to get good grades and a good education. She was not the kind of mother who would say, "I love you" to her children, but she showed her love in the way she treated us.

The first crisis of my young life was when I was three years old and I came down with malaria. My uncle took me to the clinic and the doctor said I had to take a chloropine injection, which was known as the suitable treatment for malaria. The doctor who gave me the injection managed to injure a nerve, causing partial paralysis, so that I couldn't move the left side of my body. The doctor said I would improve with mild, gradual exercise but would never be completely normal again. I wasn't able to walk at all for six months, until my father took me to a specialist in Khartoum, who had me do exercises until I was able to walk a little bit. This, of course, had a great effect on my childhood because I couldn't run and play, like a normal child. My parents chose to forgive the doctor, instead of sending him to trial. They used to say that they forgave him just like Jesus forgave us.

When I turned six, the civil war started and all southern Sudanese government employees lost their jobs. My father was one of the men laid off. Because he wanted us to continue to get a good education, he decided we had to leave Juba for Khartoum where he could arrange for another job and help us continue our schooling in better conditions than we would have in the war zone. I was happy I would get to travel by plane and live in a new place. Khartoum, being the capital of Sudan, sounded special. I thought we would have a lot of fun there.

The first thing that shocked me when I got off the plane was the weather, which in comparison to the rainy, humid climate that we were used to, was much too hot. There were also no tall trees and no green areas like the ones that surrounded our former house. Instead, we had sand yards and weather conditions so hot we couldn't play and enjoy ourselves as we had before. We lived with my uncle and his family in a house that was smaller than our home in Juba. The fact that this very large extended family was crowded in a small house meant that we had a hard time concentrating on our studies. After six months, we rented a new house when my father found a job as a member of the election committee—a well-paid job that allowed us to get new clothes and continue our education. Meanwhile, we heard bad news from our friends and relatives that people close to all of us had died in the war. The news upset me greatly and I would pray to God to end the war so we could go back to our old house and village.

My father lost his job after a year, when the election committee was eliminated, and this made life very difficult for all of us. My father had saved some money, which enabled me to finish elementary school, and later he accepted a job that paid poorly so we could continue our education. In this way I was able to finish high school. Although I frequently had the highest grades in my class, I performed poorly my last year of high school, despite studying hard, and this prevented me from following my dream of studying medicine. My mother suggested that I repeat my senior year, but I decided it would be better to study medicine abroad and so I applied for asylum through the UNHCR and waited to hear if I would be able to travel to Egypt.

My application was accepted and I set out on a most uncomfortable voyage, which took me by a two-day train trip to Halfa, by ship to Aswan, and finally, by bus to Cairo. I was stopped in Halfa because I was traveling alone, and girls were not allowed to travel without a male relative with them. Luckily, a southern man who turned out to be a friend of my father's talked to some officers and helped me get permission to continue my trip. It was 7am on a Friday morning when I arrived in Aswan and found that only Egyptians were allowed to pass. Non-Egyptians were left behind, waiting until 3pm, when the Friday prayers would end. Children were very hungry and we were all frustrated by the lack of food. To add to the frustration, when the customs officials came back at 3pm, we were told we had to take four pills if we wanted to continue to Cairo. There was no way to refuse. I don't know what was in those pills but they made me very sick. The long bus ride to Cairo was all the more miserable for me.

When I reached Cairo, I was shocked by the noise, the bright colors of billboards and neon signs, and the huge crowds, all of which I was not used to. I had cousins who taught at the St. Luanga School, in the Sacred Heart Church in Abbasiya and they sent some one to pick me up and bring me to the church compound. I went to the church at seven in the morning and I couldn't understand why people were honking their car horns so hard at that early hour.

My first days in Cairo were boring since my cousins were busy at work, so I spent my time reading books and watching television. I learned then that I was not accepted by the UNHCR as an immigrant, which meant I could not apply to the Faculty of Medicine at Cairo University. I felt like my dreams were slipping away and would never be achieved, especially after three months, when finances became more of an issue. My sister in Sweden was paying for my younger brother's education so she could not lend me any money to start my life in Cairo. I decided then to work as a babysitter, and I spent ten days with an extremely nervous woman who screamed all the time for no good reason. She shouted at her children and beat them with violent rage. I couldn't stand her and I decided to leave. She only paid me a quarter of the amount we initially agreed on and rudely ordered me out of her house.

I found another job as a personal assistant to an actress. I had to wake her up at seven every morning and make sure she stuck to her schedule. I spent the day doing various chores for her and waited for her until she came home late in the evening because that was the nature of her job. Because I worked such long hours, I could only sleep four hours a night and I quickly grew tired. When my cousin passed away, I asked for permission to take a few days off to spend time with and support my cousin. My employer refused, and since I had no choice but to go to my cousin, I left the job. I prayed to God a lot to help me find another job in order to be able to live and eat in Cairo and my prayers were answered shortly thereafter. I found work with a Muslim woman who was very kind and treated me in a civilized manner and with a respect that very few Sudanese in Egypt receive. Meanwhile, I was able to join the Faculty of Commerce at Cairo University because the department had a branch in Khartoum, and so I didn't need immigrant status to enroll. Despite it not being my chosen field, I could finally continue my studies.

I worked for two days a week from 6am to 10pm and I went to college on the other days. I had two free days during which I would study. However, school was not as pleasant as I'd hoped. Some of our lectures were held in the main branch of Cairo University, where bigoted students would try to hurt us with insults and humiliating words. I also didn't like the study of commerce because I still saw myself as a doctor. I grew up hearing my family call me "doctor," and the disappointment of not being able to fulfill my goal left me in tears a lot of the time. During my first accounting lecture, I thought, "Oh no! I am going to have to deal with numbers for four years and then for the rest of my life!" I was not at all psychologically prepared to study things I didn't like.

I always prayed to God when I was sad, and He was close enough to me that I managed to pass the first year with high grades as usual. But in my second year, I got the chance to reapply for asylum status with the UNHCR, and I spent the year believing I would be called at any time to travel to the United States or Australia. I couldn't concentrate on lectures, so I stopped attending and focused on working and saving money. Then, I learned that the UNHCR had rejected my application for the second time. Once that happened, and I realized that there was no way out, I knew that I would have to face my new life. So I started to study hard and repeated the second year. I passed and then finished my third and fourth years as well. As soon as I finished university, I decided not to work right away because I wanted to visit my family in Sudan and make sure that everyone was in good shape.

I was happy to find that my family was doing well; by renting the four-story house in Khartoum, they had a good source of income for the whole family. This money helped me on my way back to Egypt. My first thought on returning to Cairo was to help reduce the gang violence that had sprung up after the 2005 demonstration in Mustafa Mahmoud Park. When refugees realized, as I had, that their chances of resettlement were slim, and that going home was not an option despite the official peace treaty in Sudan, Sudanese youth gangs formed and began to inflict violence on one another. I felt I had to do something to end this violence; here were young people who'd escaped the horrors of violence in Sudan, who'd found sanctuary in Egypt, and were now recreating the very horrors that drove them from their home. I wanted them to stop their violent actions that were against religion, and that violated the very human rights that these young people were seeking. They were undermining their very own cause and I had to help them realize this.

I started to teach Sudanese children in church because I believe that if children are raised to learn the love of God, they won't turn to gangs. Later on, I became engaged in programs for teenagers in gangs that were designed by our church to fight gang traits. Our aim was to keep young people busy so they would have no time for violence. Our programs provided daily education, which unfortunately was not accredited by the Egyptian government. This discouraged most of our students, because they felt that their hard work was in vain. We designed music, art, and sports programs to discover the students' hidden talents and abilities. We also held parties and events and hosted plays and musical pieces, in which teenagers could showcase their talents onstage, and feel appreciated and encouraged. Our one problem was resistance on the part of some students who weren't interested in any activities, and who didn't want to leave their gangs.

It was difficult for me to understand the motivation—I couldn't understand why these teenagers would want to hurt and kill their own countrymen. Was it to feel accomplished or to gain approval, or was it deeper than that? Some of my colleagues believed that teenagers joined gangs to have money and buy expensive clothes and look well-dressed. And it was true that gang members wore expensive shoes, shirts, and pants that most refugees couldn't afford. But was style worth killing someone? And where did the money for these outfits come from in the first place? We knew that gang members stole from other refugees, but we thought it unlikely that this would raise sufficient funds to purchase the shoes, shirts, and jeans that are required attire for gang members.

One time, I talked to the head of a gang and was surprised to find out that he was kind, calm, and very intelligent. He was physically and mentally strong and the gang members would cast all their cares and worries on him.

But when I asked him why he resorted to violence, his only reply was that he would always be involved with gang "justice." He refused to disclose the source of his gang's money, and when I asked if it came from the Sudanese government, he said he didn't know.

I continued my work with teen gangs and I went to conferences and seminars that were held weekly and were responsible for generating new ideas and programs to help end gang violence in Cairo. We were attacked twice by a group of gangs during a conference in Maadi. A girl was hurt in the first attack and we took her to the hospital. I didn't understand why they attacked us since we did not belong to any gang groups. Maybe it was because we were trying to spread education and civilization to end the murder and abuse that, very possibly, they were well paid to carry out.

I have had my share of suffering, too, and I've been the victim of a great deal of discrimination. I always hear Egyptians claim that there is no racial discrimination in Cairo, but this is not true. Black-skinned African girls suffer from sexual harassment. The hurtful words thrown at me like rocks in the street remind me of how ill-mannered and uncivilized people can be. My father died after my last visit to Sudan, and I wore black to show my grief. As I was walking down the street in my mourning clothes, a man said mockingly, "Oh! Poor girl! I hope you go to visit whoever died in your family." I thought then that people have no mercy in their hearts and that they can't see that I'm a human being who is grieving for a dead family member. Another time, my sister and I were riding a bus home one day when a man sitting behind us put out his cigarette on my sister's jacket. People were screaming "Fire, fire!" and my sister was stunned and could only scream, "God help me!" until we managed to put it out. We kept the burned jacket for someone to see one day and I started to record what happened to me on a daily basis. One day, I thought, my journal of abuse will be useful. Yet despite all this I have not lost my hope and my faith.

We suffer a lot, but we know that not all people in Egypt are bad. Some cities in Egypt are beautiful. Alexandria and the North Coast are very quiet and people there are familiar with foreigners and treat us with more respect. I love the sea and the sun and I will never forget the marvelous sunset in Alexandria, which has been imprinted in my memory forever.

My journey from southern Sudan to Khartoum to Cairo and my excursion into the gang culture that is destroying the future of my country has been very difficult. I still have much to do in order to help my young Sudanese sisters and brothers to build new lives in Cairo. I believe that Cairo is a big school in which I've studied hard, facing challenge after challenge. I've learned a lot despite the pain I suffered here. Setbacks and obstacles can do two things: They can make one so angry that violence seems to be the only viable solution to the problem; or they can teach one to find a way to overcome the injustice of these challenges and turn them into valuable lessons. I learned to transcend the automatic reaction of self-pity and anger, and began to find solutions despite the seemingly endless problems of refugee life. I learned to have hope and now, as I grow older, I'm sure of one thing: God arranges whatever happens or is going to happen to me and everything is under His control, so I'm not afraid of the future. I pray to God that we can make positive changes to keep our teenagers from joining gangs, that we can end the violence that we came to Egypt to escape.

Afterword

Suad El Aasar

To many in the developed world, Sudan is just another African country plagued by war and destruction. But what Sudan has faced has been a man-slaughtering force of a twenty-year civil war that has splintered the country along geographic, ethnic, and religious lines. Over the past two decades, thousands of Sudanese have fled the country and sought refuge in neighboring countries such as Chad, Uganda, and Egypt. As an increasing number of Sudanese sought asylum in Egypt, UNHCR set up a regional office in Cairo and assumed the responsibility of determining the legal status of refugees in Egypt. Because of the UNHCR's relocation program—through which refugees, once acknowledged as legal asylum seekers, are relocated to third countries like the United States, Australia, and Canada—many asylum seekers come to Egypt in hope of being relocated. The problem, as demonstrated in the narratives, however, is that the UNHCR Regional Office in Cairo stopped registering Sudanese asylum seekers for refugee status determination interviews as of June 1, 2004, issuing refugees with yellow cards of temporary protection only. As a result of the UNHCR's halt in determination services and the subsequent standstill of refugee relocation, there may be up to three million Sudanese asylum seekers left in Egypt today.[9]

One can assume that the relocation program was put into practice to ease the responsibility placed on Egypt—a developing country in the global south with a 10 percent unemployment rate, and with 20 percent of its population living under the poverty line—in dealing with the external 'burden' of refugees. As such, and in order to determine the effectiveness of Egypt as a transit place of first asylum, it is necessary to examine the social and economic factors at play in the country as well as the historical relationship

123

between Sudan and Egypt. Until the mid-1990s, the two countries' open border policy enabled Sudanese citizens to relocate to Egypt without a residence visa. This changed in 1995, when an assassination attempt on the life of Egyptian President Mohammad Hosni Mubarak during a visit to Ethiopia was traced back to the Sudanese government. In reaction, Egypt closed its borders "and applied visa requirements on Sudanese nationals…[requiring] them to hold a residence permit"[10] and, subsequently, key issues of Sudanese refugees' lives in post-1995 Egypt have tended to focus on their legal status in relation to the UNHCR.

By the end of 2004, the UNHCR reported its recognition of 20,438 Sudanese asylum seekers as legal refugees as well as its rejection, in the period between 1997 and 2003, of 32,000 asylum seekers. Worrying as the rejection figures may be, it is equally problematic, considering the intricate tie between legal recognition by the UN organization and refugees' access to relocation and aid, that UNHCR offices only view cases that amount to approximately 10 percent of the total number of refugees living in Egypt. One wonders whether refugees have refused to file cases because they fear being rejected and deported back to Sudan, or if their cases have been filed and neglected by the UNHCR. In analyzing possible reasons behind the UNHCR's halt in determination services, Father Claudio Lurati—the Comboni priest featured in George's story and the head of Sacred Heart Church, Cairo's biggest refugee center—argues that it is a matter of political negotiation between the UNHCR and the western countries to which so many refugees aspire to relocate. This argument, also posited by Barbara Harrell-Bond, views the UNHCR as bound by western nations in attempting to reduce the number of refugees resettled in the west. As such, a vicious cycle is created in which more Sudanese refugees are drawn to Egypt in the hope of being relocated to Australia, Canada, or the United States, and more cases are rejected by the UNHCR in an attempt to limit the resettlement. The result, for many refugees, is perpetual limbo.

Employment, Economic Livelihood, and Education

Curious about how Egypt's three million guests were faring in this state of limbo, I conducted a number of interviews in al-Hayy al-Asher in Cairo. A neighborhood that serves as home to one of Cairo's largest Sudanese refugee communities, where Egyptians and Sudanese live in a working-class area, al-Hayy al-Asher is little short of a slum. Arriving in the neighborhood a few months after the Egyptian police's violent dispersion of the refugee sit-in on December 31, 2006, which left many Sudanese dead and dozens more injured, my primary focus was to investigate perceived tensions among the Sudanese and the Egyptian. In order to do this, I first interviewed a group of ten Sudanese individuals from the Hayy al-Asher area. Eight of the ten individuals were men. The interview candidates were picked at random and were between 18 and 42, with various educational backgrounds ranging from vocational school to university graduates. This group was interviewed with a primary focus on their individual perceptions of life in Egypt and the way they perceived their treatment by Egyptians. The second group consisted of ten Egyptian individuals who were also randomly picked from multiple areas. Although this group consisted of more women than men, it too varied in educational backgrounds, ranging from high school students to university graduates and with individuals ranging in age from 17 to 45 years old. The focus of the interviews held with the second sample group was to discover perceptions of, or prejudices against, the Sudanese population in Egypt.

After the interviews were held, several general areas could be categorized for analysis. For both the Sudanese and the Egyptians, a central area of concern was the availability of means of economic livelihood. While the Sudanese expressed concern with finding means for subsistence, the Egyptian sample group exhibited an additional trend of anxiety toward the presence of the Sudanese as potential threats/competition in the job market. Although not asked directly if they worried about unemployment, a good number of Egyptians voluntarily admitted their concern about the scarcity of employment opportunities, arguing that the Sudanese posed a threat in their mutual pursuit of the same job opportunities. One 17-year-old male in the Egyptian group, expected to graduate from high school shortly after the time of the interview, stated that Sudanese refugees "take residence and employment from Egyptians who can not find these things." Another 23-year-old female college graduate, unemployed at the time of the interview, echoed that sentiment, saying that the Sudanese "take up jobs and use public goods," and according to at least one other person interviewed, the Sudanese were seen as concentrating themselves ". . . in certain areas [neighborhoods]" where they "dominate things like trade in the fabric market."

The concern about Sudanese control of certain neighborhoods' econo-mies appears to be the paranoid perception of the clusters formed by the refugee community across Cairo. According to Fabienne Le Houérou, the perception of the number of Sudanese refugees in Egypt indicates Egyptian anxiety toward Sudanese presence. The author states that

> rumors around Cairo . . . suggest that [there] are 500,000 Sudanese in Arba wa Nus [an informal neighborhood]. When you compare this urban myth with concrete reality, the discrepancy is remarkable. Egyptians feel that they have been invaded because Sudanese families, in their desire to live together, occupy whole buildings. The unease felt by the Egyptians consequently leads to exaggeration of the num-ber of Sudanese. Exaggerations arise from fear. The fear of invasion is first expressed with false numbers which provide[s] a dramatic dimen-sion to the situation.[11]

In my own research, I have found that the Egyptian sample group believed there to be anywhere between thousands and five to eight million Sudanese refugees in Egypt. All but one of the interviewees also felt that the number of the Sudanese population was increasing. According to Le Houérou's study of the Arba wa Nus neighborhood, perceptions such as these are tied with assigning blame to the Sudanese for a number of very specific hardships, including the rise of rent and food prices.[12]

The reality of Sudanese refugees' employment and life in Egypt is far grimmer than the sample group interviewed might want to believe. In al-Hayy al-Asher, as in a number of neighborhoods across Cairo, the presence of Sudanese refugees is felt in barbershops, tailor shops, restaurants, tele-phone centrals, and coffee houses opened by members of the Sudanese com-munity and intended as gathering places for the refugees. While this may suggest economic independence, the shops serve a far more important socio-logical rather than financial function. In an anthropological study of Suda-nese refugees' coping mechanisms in Egypt, Stephanie I. Riak Akuei, who focuses specifically on the Dinka of southern Sudan, explains the phenom-enon of community clusters, arguing that they are formed in order to help refugees cope with the identity crisis caused by the loss of "kin, home, com-munity, and other spheres of relatedness."[13] By reforming communities in their place of asylum, the Sudanese formulate their own concepts of resilience and identity, and stress commonalities (such as love for their native land, and the oneness of the community in marriage) in order to lessen the trauma associated with relocation.

Although the community shops have helped some refugees cope with the economic setback involved in relocation, a good deal still have substantial reason to be concerned about means of economic livelihood, particularly because of the risks involved in one of the most readily available job options for refugees: housework. In her examination of Sudanese refugees' experiences in Egypt, Jane Kani Edward illuminates the negative consequences of employment in Egyptian homes on Sudanese women refugees, often the most vulnerable group in the community, arguing that "since the work done by these women is not regulated by the Egyptian government or any other labor laws, these women refugees are sometimes subjected to exploitative and humiliating work conditions."[14] These conditions include being underpaid by their employers—the presence of the Sudanese in Egypt increased the supply of house-workers, enabling Egyptians to pay less for each one—being forced to work long hours, and accepting a prescribed code of behavior while at work (many employers, for example, forbid their maids from using the family cutlery and accuse them of stealing if they attempt to leave their jobs).

The economic hardships and systematized exclusion faced by the Sudanese in Egypt often reflects most negatively on their children's education. As articulated by Edward, the increasing number of asylum seekers from Sudan, Ethiopia, and other countries forced a shift in UNHCR policies on refugees from one that promoted self-reliance through education and training programs to one that stressed basic care and maintenance instead. The shift left the Sudanese to fend for their own children's education and, while refugee children have technically been allowed into the Egyptian public school system—the only schools the refugees can afford—since 2000, in practice, the schools' requirements for acceptance deem the enrollment of Sudanese children impossible. As pointed out by Edward, the schools' insistence on the provision of children's previous school records and birth certificates are impractical considering that most children relocate to Egypt directly from internally displaced people (IDP) camps. Furthermore, the schools' policy of only accepting students with *iqamas*, or residence permits, places an additional financial burden on refugee families, many of whom cannot afford the paperwork required to obtain the permits. For many, learning centers and schools operated by churches for the benefit of refugee children become the only alternative, but considering both the overcrowding in the schools and the fact that the certificates they issue are not recognized by either the Egyptian or the Sudanese governments, it is not surprising to find that "the church groups supporting the refugees [estimate] two-thousand refugee children to be without schooling."[15]

Racial Discrimination

More than concerns about economic livelihood, the most common grievances expressed by the Sudanese refugees interviewed in al-Hayy al-Asher were complaints of discrimination and racism. One Sudanese man interviewed reported being called *asmar,* the Arabic equivalent of 'darky,' and another young man complained of the association of the Sudanese with animals, saying "we get called things like 'black dog.'" These complaints echo the patterns of discrimination identified by Edward, who, in her examination of racism and sexual harassment against Sudanese women, makes a distinction between the way lighter-skinned women of northern Sudan, who are viewed as Arab, and darker-skinned women of the south, who are viewed as African, are treated. Maintaining that the basis for racism could be found in Egypt's historic enslavement of the southern Sudanese, Edward argues that they are seen as "different culturally, linguistically, and religiously . . . [viewed] as inferiors both racially and culturally."[16] Edward, who also mentions women's complaints of being called 'darky,' links the racist attitudes to incidents of sexual harassment that include being followed on the street, groped, and/or propositioned for sex.[17]

In an effort to ascertain the degree of racism found in the general Egyptian opinion, I analyzed the interviews carried out with the Egyptian interview group for any sort of embedded prejudice. One 22-year-old Egyptian male, an engineering student, explained the police brutality in the December 31 incident by saying that "Egyptian soldiers are usually uneducated, and to them the physical blackness of the Sudanese probably represented things like disease and burden." When asked why he thought the color of their skin would be associated with disease and burden in the minds of the soldiers, he replied "black has always been a depressing color and I guess that's just what people come to think." A middle aged woman interviewed also offered the following analogy: "If you have someone who is a guest in your home who is constantly causing trouble, and you do not kick him out, what are you supposed to do?" When further asked if she considered the Sudanese to be troublemakers, the woman claimed no knowledge of their residence patterns in Egypt but, with increasingly visible anger, advised that the Sudanese need to "be respectable and not cause problems" if they wanted a solution to their problems.

Clearly there are two general trends reciprocated in both sample groups: mutual pursuit of scarce means of economic livelihood, and evidence of racial discrimination against the Sudanese population in Egypt and there is a substantial connection to be underscored between the two. According to Lincoln Quillian, prejudice is a response to threats to established group privileges and, in the case at hand, Egyptian anxiety about the presence of the Sudanese in the job market can be seen to support Quillian's view of prejudice as a response to perceived threats to the dominant group by a subordinate one.[18]

Although issues of racism in Egypt are not likely to be resolved with any one study, our hope is that this project will work toward eliminating some of the fear ingrained in the mainstream Egyptian mentality regarding Sudanese refugees. Faced, as they are, with discrimination, harsh economic situations, and little chance of relocation, the Sudanese refugee community is in dire need of help. Universal moral standards and human rights must demand that something be done about those left in limbo, in a country that often cannot feed itself.

References

"Causes and Consequences" available from http://www.forcedmigration. org/guides/fmo029/fmo029-3.htm (accessed on April 12, 2006).

Edward, Jane Kani. *Sudanese Women Refugees: Transformations and Future Imaginings.* New York: Palgrave Macmillan, 2007.

Le Houérou, Fabienne "Living with Your Neighbour: Forced Migrants and their Hosts in an Informal Area of Cairo, Arba wa Nus," *Diaspora in Cairo: Transient Presence and Transit Territory Conference* (2004). Cairo, Egypt: CEDEJ, AUC FMRS Department.

Quillian, Lincoln. "Prejudice as a Response as Perceived Group Threat: Population Composition and Anti-Immigrant and Racial Prejudice in Europe," American Sociological Review (1995): 586–611.

Riak Akuei, Stephanie I. "Cultural Mindfulness amongst the Dinka Displaced by War: Cairo as Potent Place to Points Beyond," from http://www.aucegypt.edu/fmrs/Research/Akuei.pdf (accessed April 18, 2006).

Notes

1   Turkey and Iraq were the two other governments.
2   Most ratifying states allow refugees to work immediately, although some require that they have been resident for three years before allowing them to work. After the three years, refugees should not have to have a work permit.
3   The Cessation Clause of the 1951 Geneva Treaty allows a host state to declare conditions in the home state are 'okay,' so that refugees must return there.
4   In 2006, a group of almost 3,000 Sudanese refugees assembled in front of Mustafa Mahmoud Mosque, Cairo, to protest their living conditions and limited opportunities. The park is located near the offices of the United Nations Higher Commissioner for Refugees (UNHCR). After three months of camping, the protests were broken up by security forces. The violence resulted in 27 deaths and injury and detention of hundreds.
5   See note in Foreword.
6   For more background, see Foreword.
7   For more background, see Foreword.
8   WFP: World Food Program, UNICEF: United Nations International Children's Emergency Fund, FAO: Food and Agriculture Organization, SCF: Save the Children Fund.
9   See "Causes and Consequences," http://www.forcedmigration.org/guides/fmo029/fmo029-3.htm (accessed on April 12, 2006).
10   "Causes and Consequences" available from http://www.forcedmigration.org/guides/fmo029/fmo029-3.htm (accessed on April 12, 2006).
11   Fabienne Le Houérou (2004) "Living with Your Neighbour: Forced Migrants and their Hosts in an Informal Area of Cairo, Arba wa Nus" *Diaspora in Cairo: Transient Presence and Transit Territory Conference.* Cairo, Egypt: CEDEJ, AUC FMRS Department.
12   Ibid.
13   Stephanie I. Riak Akuei, "Cultural Mindfulness Amongst The Dinka Displaced By War: Cairo As Potent Place To Points Beyond." (Unpublished) Retrieved April 18, 2006, from http://www.aucegypt.edu/fmrs/Research/Akuei.pdf.
14   Jane Kani Edward, *Sudanese Women Refugees: Transformations and Future Imaginings* (New York: Palgrave Macmillan, 2007), 172.
15   Ibid, 106.
16   Edward, *Sudanese Women Refugees: Transformations and Future Imaginings,* 182.
17   Ibid, 183.
18   Lincoln Quillian. "Prejudice as a Response as Perceived Group Threat: Population Composition and Anti-Immigrant and Racial Prejudice in Europe," American Sociological Review (1995): 586.